Book 1 Oxford Social Geographies

Martin Simons

Poverty and Wealth in Cities and Villages

Studies in Ghana
Kenya
Northern India
Singapore
South America
Australia

1972 Oxford University Press

Acknowledgements

We are grateful to the following for permission to reproduce photographs:–

Author, page 48, 53 right and bottom left, 106 top, 107 right, 109 left, 119, 121, 122, 123, 125, 126, 127, 128; Australian News and Information Bureau, 106 bottom, 107 left, 109 right; Colin Ballantyne and Partners, 117; Cadbury Bros. Ltd., 28 left; Camera Press, 4, 5, 6, 7, 21, 26 top, 27 left, 29, 40, 41, 42, 43 bottom left, 53 top left, 54, 55, 66, 83 bottom, 85 bottom right, 101 right; D. Darian Smith, 116; David Crease, 100 bottom; Department of Lands, South Australia, 111; East African Railways and Harbours, 31 top, 35 top, 36 top; Food and Agricultural Organisation of the United Nations, 61, 64, 65, 69, 89, 90, 91; Derick Garnier, 67 top and bottom right; The Geographical Magazine, 32 bottom left and right; Ghana Information Service, 20 bottom, 22, 23, 24 top, 26 bottom, 27, 31; Government Information Centre, Singapore, 85 top and bottom left and bottom right; P. G. Greenwood, 80 bottom; Colin Henfrey, 100 top, 101 left, 102, 103; R. D. Hill, 83 top; John Hillelson Agency, 44 top, 95; Journal of Tropical Geography, 79, 80 top, 81; Victor Kennett, 74, 75; Kenya Information Service, 31 bottom, 32 top left and right, 34, 35 bottom, 36 bottom, 37, 38, 39; D. N. Lester, 16, 24 bottom; The Mount Everest Foundation, 66; Mr. Six Photo Service, 20; Ostman Agency, 94; OUP Ghana Branch, 11, 28 right; Oxfam, 67 bottom left; South Australian Housing Trust, 115; Syndication International, 43 top left; Tata Iron and Steel Company Ltd., 70; Mrs. Rhonda B. Toussaint, 131, 133, 134; World Health Organisation, 43 top right, 44 bottom, 45, 52.
Fig. 4 was drawn by B. E. Nicholson.
We regret we have been unable to trace the copyright holders for the photographs on pages 48, 53 top right, bottom left and right.

Oxford University Press, Ely House, London W.1
GLASGOW NEW YORK TORONTO MELBOURNE WELLINGTON
CAPE TOWN IBADAN NAIROBI DAR ES SALAAM LUSAKA ADDIS ABABA
DELHI BOMBAY CALCUTTA MADRAS KARACHI LAHORE DACCA
KUALA LUMPUR SINGAPORE HONG KONG TOKYO

Photoset by BAS Printers Limited, Wallop, Hampshire
and printed in Great Britain at the University Press, Oxford
by Vivian Ridler, Printer to the University

Contents

	Introduction	5
1	Hungry Season in Northern Ghana	8
2	Developing Ghana	18
3	Farming in the Highlands of Kenya	30
4	Some Cities of Northern India	40
5	Villages in Bihar, Northern India	56
6	Homes in Singapore	77
7	Changes in Chilean Farming	86
8	Growing Cities of South America	92
	Notes on Planned cities	104
9	City with a Plan	106
10	Fruit Growers in South Australia	119
11	Poverty in Australia	131
	Postscript	135
	Index	136

Photo. 1 A hillside village near Rio de Janiero. Rich or poor?

Introduction

This is a book of comparisons and contrasts. As you read each chapter you should compare the places described with others which are dealt with in the other chapters, and with other areas which you know of, including your home district. The examples in this book have been taken from the southern continents of Africa, South America, Australia, and the sub-continent of India.

Even in one district or within one country there are great differences between one place and another and also between one group of people and another. The contrasts you will discover in this book are mainly between city districts and country areas. There are wealthy people in the cities and in the country; there are poor in both also. As you read you should try to understand how these differences have arisen and develop ideas about how some of the resulting problems might be solved.

The questions which you will find every now and then throughout the book are for you to think and talk about with your friends and your teacher. Sometimes you might become sufficiently interested in one of these questions to make some notes about it, or follow it up further with some more reading or study. To begin with, two very important questions appear on the next two pages, with some notes. Some things to do are also suggested. These will help with the rest of the book.

Photo. 2 São Paulo town centre. Some people living here are wealthy, but is everyone in such a city rich?

Photo. 3 Outside an Indian house. A bull is used to work this mill which is crushing oil out of seeds. Do you suppose such a house contains many luxuries?

List of items

a house to live in
a television
a washing machine
a motor car
a sailing dinghy
a radio set
household tools
fresh bread daily
medicines
milk delivered daily
a caravan
a camera
watches and clocks
a record player
a vegetable garden
chairs and tables
a refrigerator
shoes
two good meals per day
books
floor carpets
warm clothing
a second car
sporting equipment
clean water on tap
a bicycle
cooking utensils
jewellery
tailored suits
cosmetics

How can we measure wealth and poverty?

At first we say, a rich man has much money, a poor one has little. But money alone is not really worth anything—we cannot eat it, wear it, or make it into anything very useful. We value money only because we can buy things with it, or pay rent, fares, and so on. A rich family can buy almost anything they want. A very poor family might be unable to buy anything at all. Some things are absolutely necessary for life; food and drink, shelter, and usually clothing. Food is the most necessary of all things; some people are so poor that they do not even get enough food. On the other hand, things like jewellery, sweets, toys, cigarettes, etc., are not necessary at all. We could live without them; they are luxuries. In between luxuries and necessities are a great many things that are not absolutely needed but often it would be very hard to get on without them.

On the left is a list of some items that might belong or be available to an ordinary family in Britain or any wealthy country. See if you can arrange them in order of importance—necessities at the top of your list, luxuries at the bottom. You will probably find you have quite an argument about the ones in between.

Photo. 4 A modern machine tool factory in Bangalore, India. Work in a factory means at least some regular wages to buy necessities.

What are the main differences between life in towns and life in country districts?

In towns a great many people live close together; their houses stand side by side or they live in tall blocks of flats or tenements. In the country they are farther apart. Most country people work on farms or sometimes as quarrymen or miners. In towns most people work in factories, offices, shops or other places where large numbers of workers have to come together.

A countryman might visit a town to buy goods he could not get near his home. He would probably have to come to town to visit a theatre or large hospital, and to sell the produce from his land. His children might have to go to town to attend secondary school or to go to college.

A town dweller might go to the country for a holiday to escape the noise and bustle. Some people who work in town like to have their homes in the country so they travel every day to work. They are called commuters.

How far would you have to travel to visit the places listed below?

a farm	a large factory
a big supermarket	a hospital
a mine or quarry	a theatre
an airport	a fruit orchard
a college or university	a butcher's shop
a toy shop	a police station
a court house	a flour mill
a cinema	a block of flats
a water reservoir	a bus depot
a cattle market	a cathedral

an area of woodland or moorland

1 Hungry Season in Northern Ghana

Fig. 1 Africa showing the position of Ghana

Weights

One way of finding out if a person is getting enough to eat is to weigh him from time to time. You have probably seen this done to a baby; we expect all healthy children to get heavier as they grow, and if they do not, something has to be done about it. You probably know plenty of people, particularly young women, who take a great deal of trouble not to eat too much, because they do not want to become overweight. If ever you try to take out an insurance policy on your life, you will find the policy will cost you more if you are seriously overweight for your age and height. The insurance company doctors have tables like the ones shown on the next page which give the normal weights of men and women in Britain. These tables allow for differences between the sexes and also for different heights. A tall man is likely to weigh more than a short one, for instance.

People who have been seriously ill for a long time often lose weight, but when they recover they soon see a difference on the scales. Putting on weight is a sign of their being well again. Very old people lose weight too, and you may read sometimes of a professional boxer who has to go on a diet so that he can get his weight down to the class in which he wants to box. Jockeys sometimes do the same to avoid overloading their horses. But most ordinary people are about the average weight; a little above or below it. Many doctors think people in wealthy countries like Britain, U.S.A., Australia, Canada, and others, eat too much.

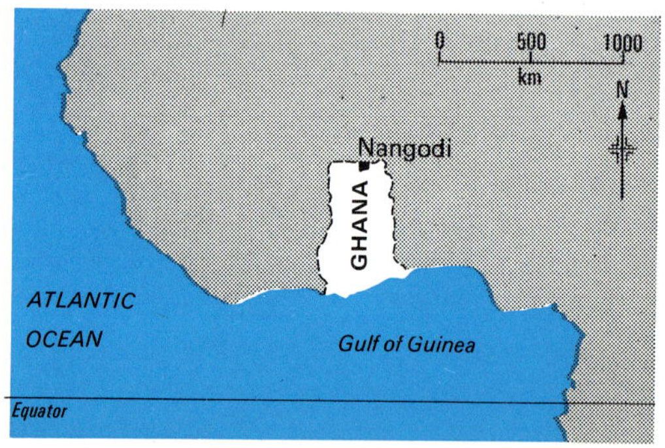

Fig. 2 Sketch map of West Africa showing the position of Nangodi in Ghana

Look at the figures in the second table. These were obtained by weighing a number of people in a district known as Nangodi, in northern Ghana. The sketch map (Fig. 2) shows where this is in West Africa.

Use your atlas or wall map to locate Nangodi exactly, and use the school globe to find out how far from your home Nangodi is.

Average weights of men in Britain

Height in centimetres	Weight in kilogrammes
152 cm	57 kg
155 cm	59 kg
158 cm	60 kg
160 cm	61 kg
163 cm	63 kg
165 cm	64 kg
168 cm	65 kg
171 cm	68 kg
173 cm	70 kg
175 cm	71 kg
178 cm	73 kg
180 cm	75 kg
183 cm	78 kg
185 cm	81 kg
187 cm	83 kg
190 cm	86 kg

Average weights of men in Nangodi

Height in centimetres	Weight in kilogrammes December	June
165 cm	57 kg	54 kg
168 cm	59 kg	55 kg
171 cm	60 kg	57 kg
173 cm	61 kg	57 kg

The tables are not so long as those for British men and women, because not many very tall or short people were weighed. Note: these weights are averages and do not necessarily represent 'ideal' or 'correct' weights. Notice that the people of Nangodi were weighed twice, in December and in June.

Average weights of women in Britain

Height in centimetres	Weight in kilogrammes
142 cm	51 kg
145 cm	52 kg
147 cm	53 kg
150 cm	54 kg
152 cm	55 kg
155 cm	56 kg
158 cm	58 kg
160 cm	60 kg
163 cm	62 kg
165 cm	63 kg
168 cm	64 kg
171 cm	65 kg
173 cm	68 kg
175 cm	70 kg
178 cm	71 kg
180 cm	73 kg
183 cm	75 kg

Average weights of women in Nangodi

Height in centimetres	Weight in kilogrammes December	June
152 cm	44.5 kg	43 kg
155 cm	52 kg	48 kg
158 cm	52 kg	48.5 kg
160 cm	52 kg	49 kg

Write down the average weight of a British man 168 centimetres tall. Next to it write down the weight in December of a 168 centimetres man in Nangodi. Then write down the Nangodi man's weight for June. Do the same for women of 158 centimetres.

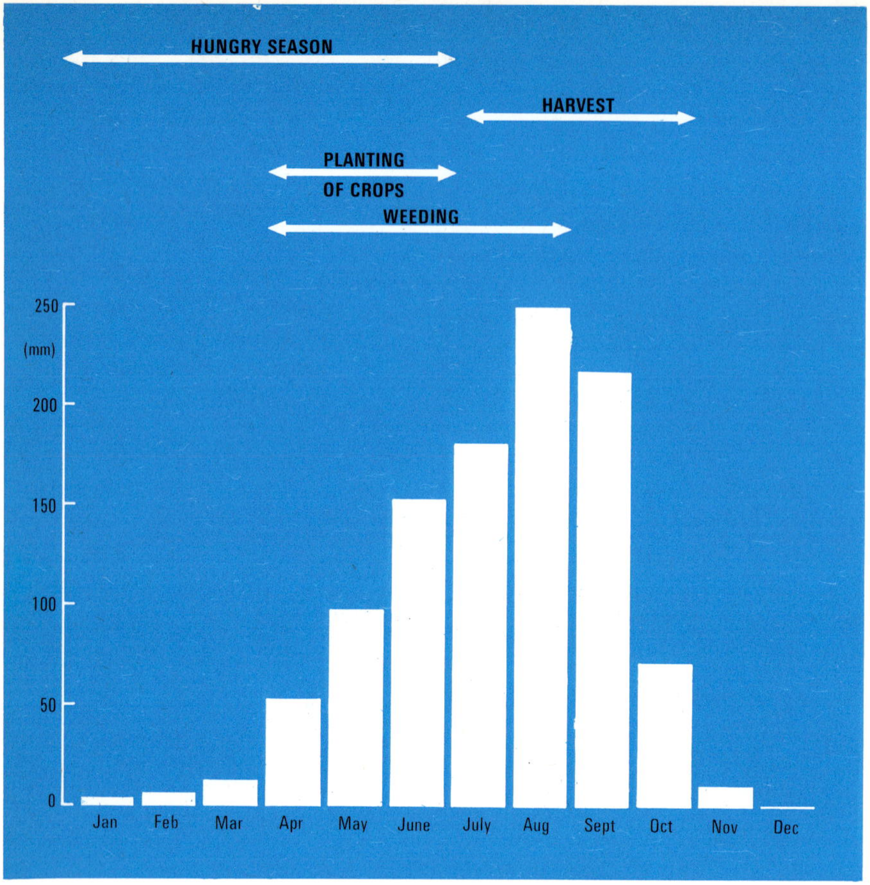

Fig. 3 Rainfall and work in Nangodi, an average year

This difference in the weights could be because people in wealthy countries eat too much, or it might be that those in Nangodi do not get enough food. What do the June Nangodi weights suggest about the food supply in Nangodi at that time of year?

There are two important things to remember about these figures. First, the Nangodi folk are nearly always thinner than Europeans. This might be because they are always working very hard, and perhaps they eat less too. Secondly, they lose weight at certain times of year.

Photo. 5 Farmer sitting in front of a corn-silo in northern Ghana

Rain and crops

In Fig. 3 there are some figures of rainfall at different times of year in Nangodi. The diagram also shows the work that the people do as the year goes on.

Use Fig. 3 to answer these questions:

Which month has the greatest rainfall? Which has the least? Is December a dry month or a wet one? What work are the people doing at that time of year? What do you know about their weight at that season? Can you think of reasons why they may be heavier in December than in June?

The graph shows only one year—on the next page you will find one which shows rainfall for a period of several years (Fig. 5).

Write a paragraph about each of these subjects:

(1) The weights of people in Nangodi in December and in June.

(2) Wet and dry times of year.

(3) Work done by the people at different times of the year.

In Nangodi there are no villages. Each family has its own farm, set away from other farms, and they grow nearly all their food in the fields nearby. They have a little extra land in the 'bush' (wild) country some

way off.

The crops grown are chiefly millet (Guinea corn), and groundnuts (Fig. 4).

Many families have some chickens, guinea fowl, goats, and sheep. But none of these are used as food, except occasionally in religious ceremonies as sacrifices. Even if a family is very short of food indeed, they will sell their animals in exchange for millet rather than eat them. Other ways by which they may get some extra money are by gathering firewood in the bush, or by making baskets for sale in the local market.

They will sell their animals only when their own granary is getting empty. In October, November, and December, the harvest is gathered in. At this time of year the granary should be full.

Fig. 4a Millet (Guinea corn) plants and life-size detail of part of an ear of millet showing large grains which produce nourishing white meal

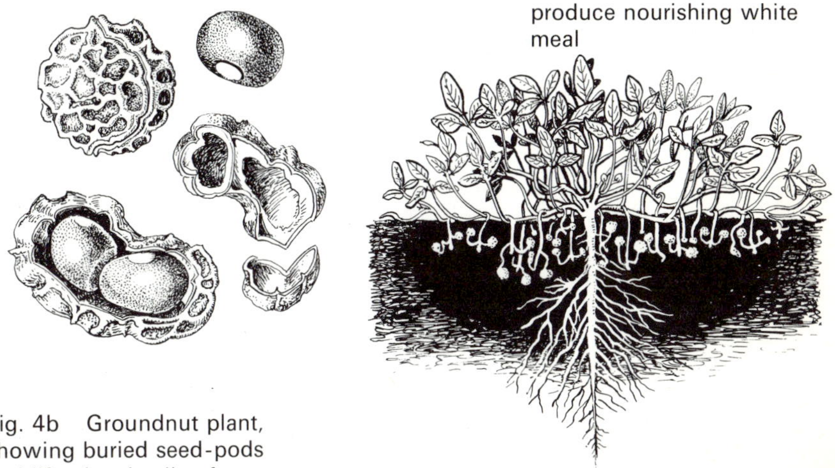

Fig. 4b Groundnut plant, showing buried seed-pods and life-size details of two types of groundnuts

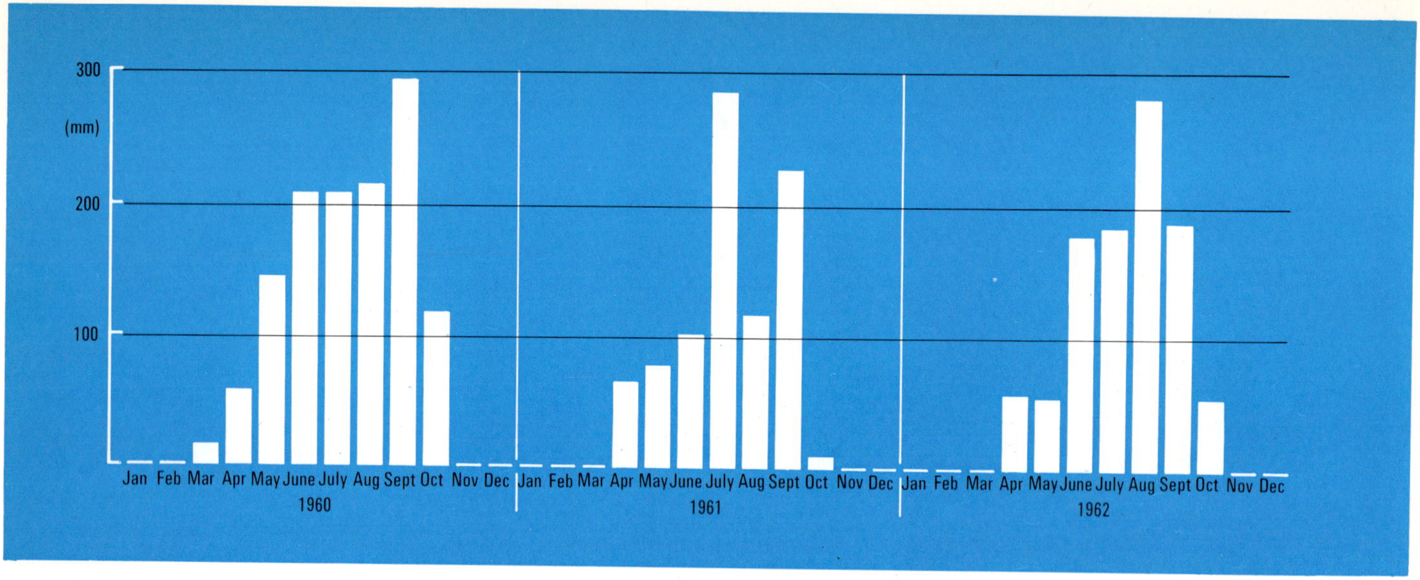

Fig. 5 Rainfall in Nangodi from January 1960 to December 1962

Study the diagram showing rainfall in Nangodi in the three years 1960, 1961, 1962 (Fig. 5). 1960 was a good year. There was plenty of rain while the crops were growing, so the harvest was good. Even so, most families had emptied their granaries by February and March of the next year. They had to sell some of their animals. Work out and write down some reasons why it is especially important for the men to have plenty of food to eat just at that time of year. Now examine what happened in 1961. Write down the names of each month from April to October. Then compare each month's rainfall, and write down 'more', 'less', or 'about the same' according to whether the month in 1961 was wetter or drier than the same month of the previous year. Would Nangodi families be more or less hungry in 1961 than in 1960? What would happen to a family that had sold all its animals in the previous year?

The Dry Season

The map (Fig. 6) will help you to find out why there is such a dry season each year. To the south of Nangodi lies an area of forest where there is rain all the year round. The winds blowing off the Gulf of Guinea bring the water which has evaporated from the ocean. Almost every day, there are large, billowing clouds which often build up into thunderstorms, and the rain comes regularly. Trees are very tall. The climate is hot as well as wet, which encourages plant growth. Far to the north of Nangodi lies the Sahara Desert. This is an area with very little rain. The air is dry and there are few clouds to keep the heat of the sun off.

In Europe, and in Canada and Russia, winter weather tends to be cold because the sun is lower in the sky during the day and the nights are long. Cold air comes in from the north. In summer the sun is higher, nights are shorter, and warmer air comes from the south. In Nangodi, the sun is always high in the sky because the area lies in the tropics. The days and nights are not very different in length. But once again, in winter the air tends to come from the north, and in summer it comes mainly from the south. This means dry, Sahara desert air from November to March. The rains begin when the moist air from the ocean arrives. The change from one kind of air to another is sometimes slow and gradual, but often it is fairly rapid with rough winds and heavy clouds. After months without any rain, thunder clouds begin to appear and they get more and more frequent as the days go by. But thunderstorms are 'chancy'. There may be a storm in one place while a few kilometres away no rain comes.

The rainfall is not very reliable. In some years the moist, oceanic air may reach Nangodi earlier than usual, and remain over the district longer than expected. This will probably mean a good year, with more rain and good crops. Even then, often there is not enough food at the end of the year.

At other times the Saharan air may linger over the country till April and arrive again early in October. This is likely to be a bad year. All will be hungry and many may die.

Fig. 6 The climate zones of Africa

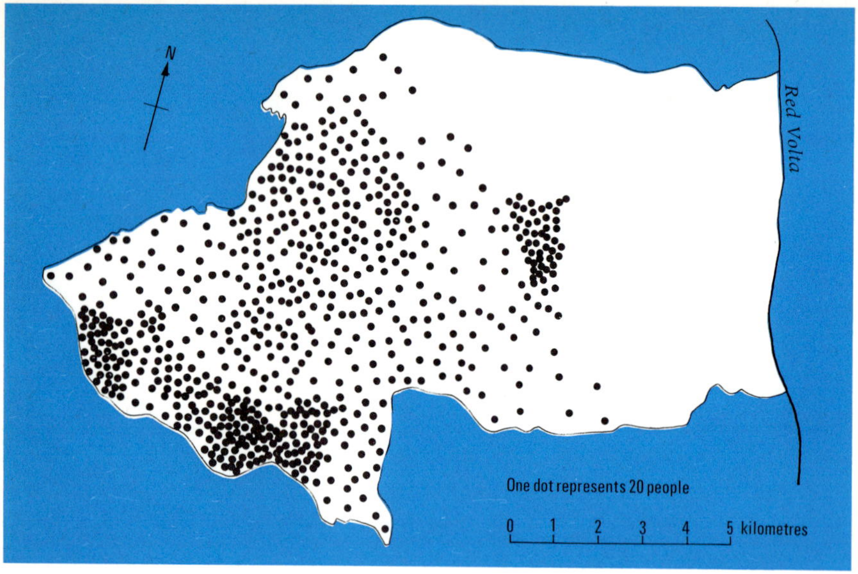

Fig. 7 Population map of Nangodi

The map (Fig. 6) shows that there are many other areas in Africa where the climate is similar to that in Nangodi. Although the people of these other areas are different from the Nangodi in many ways, they nearly always depend on the rainy season to water their fields, and like the Nangodi, they are often hungry.

Trace or copy the map showing other parts of Africa which have the same kind of 'hot, wet, and dry' climate.

In your school atlas find a map of the world showing other similar climates in South and Central America, India and south-east Asia, and Australia. They are usually called 'Savanna' climates.

The Nangodi are poor. Is there any way they could become wealthy?

The map (Fig. 7) shows Nangodi on a large scale. The eastern boundary of the district is the river Red Volta. The population of the whole district is about 14 000 people. On the map the areas where they live are marked by dots according to the numbers in each section. What do you notice about the part of Nangodi nearest to the river?

One way of increasing the amount of food in Nangodi would be to farm more land. The map shows that there is a very large area of land which is not occupied and where there are no farms. Why do the people not enlarge their fields and farms by using this waste land?

Farm work is all done by hand. They have no tractors or other machinery to do the heavy work. In the wet season everything grows very rapidly, including weeds. If weeds are left to grow they soon choke the millet and corn crops. The family have to work sometimes twelve hours a day for weeks on end just to keep the weeds down. They do the weeding with short-handled hoes, working in a stooping position. It is back-breaking toil. To take on more land would be impossible in these conditions.

Can you suggest ways of making the

work of the Nangodi people easier? If your ideas were to be carried out, would they cost anything? Could the Nangodi pay?

Diseases

The other important reason why the eastern part of Nangodi is left empty is because people living there become sick. There is a disease called 'river blindness' which is caused by tiny worms in the blood. The worms are passed from one person or animal's bloodstream to another when they are bitten by a small, black fly which lives and breeds near to rivers in this part of Africa. The fly lays its eggs in fast, running water, and people going into the eastern area are often bitten on the legs by the flies, which feed on blood. After being infected, the sick person's skin develops thick and dry patches, and small lumps, called nodules, appear. The disease spreads gradually up from the legs until after months, or even years in some cases, it affects the eyes and causes blindness. Because of river blindness, eastern Nangodi is not safe to live or work in. The flies can travel several kilometres from the river, so that even in the inhabited districts there are many cases of river blindness.

If a person has enough of the right kind of food to eat, he has a good chance of recovering from a serious disease. His body is strong and healthy, and sometimes even without a doctor he gets better. But the Nangodi people who catch river blindness are not well fed and their resistance is low.

Perhaps the diseases could be got rid of by poisoning the water in which the black flies lay their eggs. The government of Ghana has done this, but the flies still manage to find places, inside creeks and small tributary streams, where the eggs can hatch and the grubs live until they change into flies. Also the poisoning has to be repeated often if the flies are to be kept away for good. Another way of helping is to inject people with drugs which kill the worms in the blood. Now drugs are available and many of the Nangodi have been cured.

If river blindness can be overcome, the new land must be farmed with modern tools and up-to-date methods. If this is not done, soil erosion is likely, and this would lead to a worse situation than before. They might get rid of the birds that eat the millet in the fields and the pests that steal food out of the granaries after it has been stored. These and other ideas all require the understand-

Photo. 6 Homes in the upper Volta district of northern Ghana

ing and co-operation of the Nangodi people themselves. The children rarely or never go to school, so hardly anyone can read and write, or understand how to use modern machinery and fertilizers on their farms. To improve conditions, schools, teachers, doctors, and experts on farming are needed to teach people how to grow more food. The government of Ghana is doing what it can to help in these ways.

You will now be able to answer these questions:

Are the Nangodi rich? (Look back at the list of possessions on page 6, and your own list of necessities and luxuries.)

Do the Nangodi have all the necessities? Do they have any luxuries?

Does what you have learned in this chapter change your ideas about wealth and poverty at all? If so, how are your ideas different now?

Nangodi houses

Each Nangodi house belongs to a particular family. It consists of a series of circular huts, each of which is like a separate room with a courtyard outside and possibly walls to screen the courtyard. There is an outer wall built to enclose the whole house. (See Fig. 8 opposite and Photo. 6 above.)

Fig. 8 Plan of typical house in Nangodi

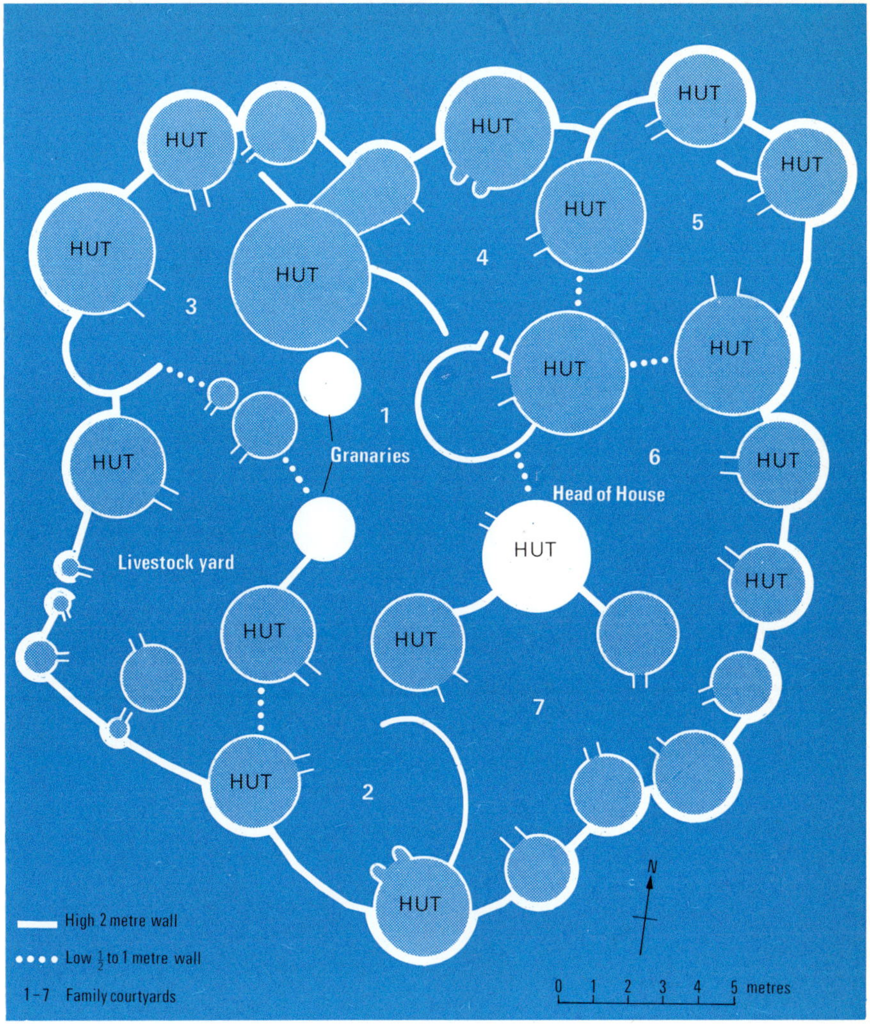

The head of the family has more than one wife. He has a hut-room in the middle of the house, with a central courtyard. Each of his wives has a separate hut with its own courtyard; his sons will have hut-rooms added and when they marry their wives also will have rooms of their own. As the family gets larger more huts are built, but each son, with his wives, lives in a separate group of huts around a courtyard. The larger the family, the bigger the house. When the head of the family dies his oldest son will usually take over his hut; the other sons may move away to build separate houses somewhere else in Nangodi. What would happen if the family was not getting enough food? What would happen to a family that grew large without farming more land?

Manure from the cattle owned by the family is allowed to collect in the cattle yard (where the cows are penned up at night). Early in the rainy season the manure is taken out in baskets and spread on the farm land. The more cattle the family have, the better their crops.

What would happen if a family had sold nearly all its cattle? Why do they sometimes sell their cattle? (See pages 11–12.)

2 Developing Ghana

Roads and railways

Three maps of Ghana are drawn below. They show how roads have developed in Ghana since the year 1900. In 1900 they were only rather narrow tracks kept clear of bushes and trees, but without any special surface. In wet weather they were very muddy and in the dry season became dusty. The graph of rainfall in South Ghana shows in which month of the year the roads would be wettest (Fig. 10). Compare the seasons with those of Nangodi in the previous chapter. In places where there were no roads, the only means of travelling about

Fig. 9a, b, c Developing roads in Ghana

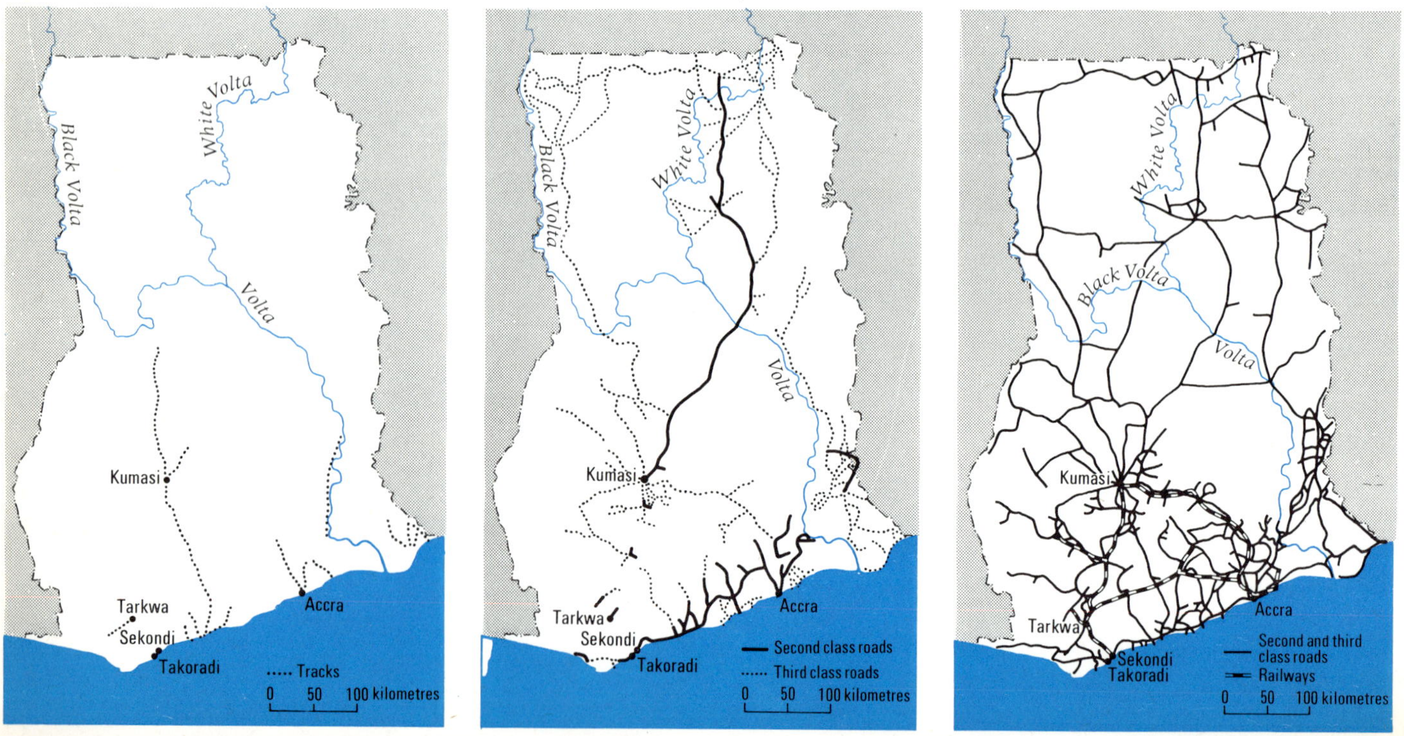

was on foot along narrow paths. These paths were called 'hammock tracks' because they were just wide enough for a man to be carried along in a hammock on a wooden pole between two bearers. The 1900 map shows no roads at all in northern Ghana.

Make a tracing of the map of Ghana's forest zone (Fig. 11) and lay it over the map of roads (Fig. 9). Then compare the graphs of rainfall in North and South Ghana (Figs. 3 and 10).

Even on the later maps the northern parts of Ghana seem to have very few roads compared with the south. Nearly all the first class roads—broad, modern highways with good, metalled surfaces, capable of taking motor cars and heavy trucks and lorries in all weathers, are in the south.

The river Volta, with its main tributaries, the Black and White Voltas, were always important routes. But these rivers had many rapids and rocky sections, so that although they were wide and in some places deep, there was never any traffic of big ships or paddle-steamers. There was quite a lot of canoe traffic and in the north this was the only means of getting about other than riding or walking.

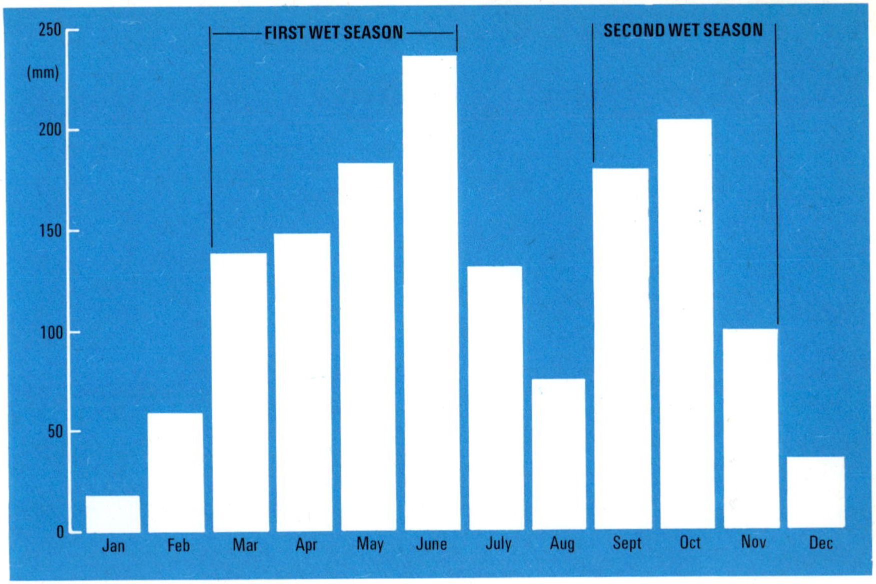

Fig. 10 Graph of rainfall at Kumasi in the forest regions of Ghana. Which is the driest month?

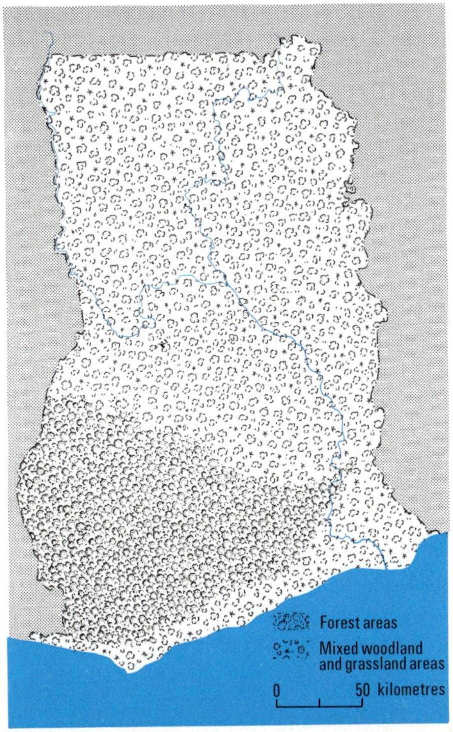

Fig. 11 The main forest and savanna regions of Ghana

Photo. 7 Street scene in Kumasi

Photo. 9 Railway station. Passengers buy refreshments for the 200-mile journey from Accra to Takoradi. The goods for sale are carried on trays balanced on the womens' heads in the traditional African fashion.

Photo. 8 A country road

The first railway to be completed was a line from Sekondi to Tarkwa, in 1901. A great deal of money was spent on this.

At many places in this part of West Africa the early European traders had discovered gold, and this first railway was built to allow mining machinery to be carried to Tarkwa, where new gold mines were opened. When the line was extended to Kumasi, the trains began to carry passengers as well as goods. The railway proved useful to the people of Ghana in many ways although it was originally built for the gold mining.

The map (Fig. 11) shows that this region is forested (see also the map of Africa, Fig. 6), and soon the trains began to carry fine African timbers from the forests down the coast for shipment and sale in Britain. Two other important things were soon going by rail to the coast—palm oil and cocoa.

Kumasi

Before the railway, Kumasi was already an important centre; it was the capital town of the Ashanti people who had ruled the central, forested regions of Ghana. People came to the market in the town to sell their goods, and these would then be carried down to the coast and on from there to Britain. Usually the barrels of palm oil or cocoa beans would be rolled along the forest tracks from the villages and farms and then would be loaded into the trains. The only other way of carrying goods was by 'head loading', that is, carrying packages on the head. This is still a common sight in many African countries.

Cocoa for drinking and making choclate became popular in Europe and America and many plantations of cocoa trees grew up in Ghana. Rolling barrels full of cocoa along a forest track is impossible unless the track is kept clear and reasonably level. This is how many roads near Kumasi began. Barrel-rolling tracks through the forest became wider and busier, and Kumasi became the centre of a road network. Reliable motor vehicles arrived in the Gold Coast in the 1920s and the roads had to be widened and surfaced.

102

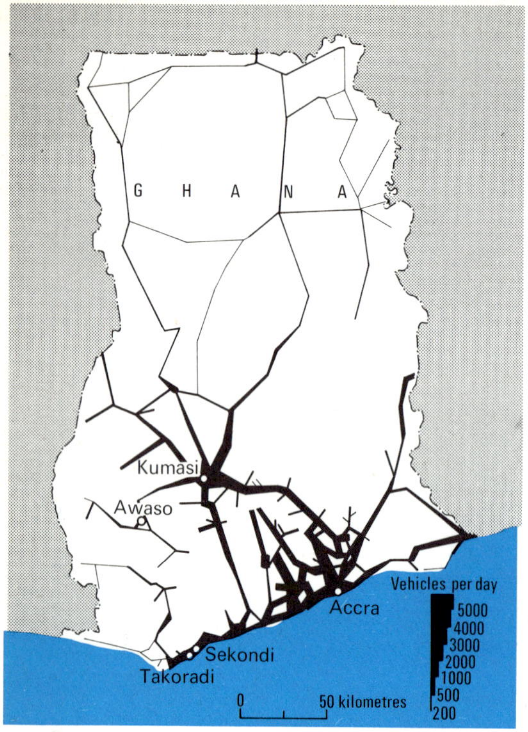

Fig. 12 Traffic flow in Ghana

Accra

Kumasi was not the only important centre in the Gold Coast. Notice that in 1900 there were already two roads running northwards from Accra on the coast.

Accra was chosen as the capital of the British Gold Coast government. One reason for this choice was that Accra was free of the tsetse fly, a pest which, like the black fly of Nangodi, carries disease and affects both men and cattle. At Accra it was possible to use animals for riding and pulling carts; the tsetse fly prevented this in most areas. Within a few years the town had grown quite large.

Accra has continued to grow. It is now the largest city in Ghana.

Notice on Fig. 9c how the road pattern around Accra spreads out in all directions now, and links up with Kumasi's similar network. Fig. 12 shows the present traffic flow on the main roads of Ghana. On this a road is drawn wide or narrow according to the amount of traffic it carries each day, as the key shows. The road from Accra to Kumasi is very busy. What about the roads from Sekondi to Kumasi? The railway is still working, of course. What can you say about traffic in northern Ghana?

Make a traffic flow map of the roads near your school and compare it with this map of Ghana.

Both Sekondi and Accra had a serious problem. There was no proper harbour.

Photo. 10 Accra—market

Photo. 11 Modern methods of loading ships have replaced the old surfboats at Tema Harbour.

Ships had to anchor a kilometre or two off the shore. Then large boats had to be paddled out from the beach to tie alongside and the cargoes from the holds were lifted out of the ship and lowered by ship's derrick crane into the boat. When full, the boat was rowed ashore until it could be beached safely and unloaded. Often the waves on the beach were high and the boats had to be skilfully managed to avoid their being upset or sunk by the surf. On one occasion when a railway locomotive had been sent all the way from England by ship, in parts, to be assembled at Accra, the whole lot, except one axle and two wheels, was lost in the sea. To calm the surf, large breakwaters were built, but the cargoes still had to be unloaded into boats and when the time came for a shipload of cocoa to be sent off, the surf boats once more had to carry each sackful through the waves to the steamer. Many times a whole boatload would be upset and ruined by salt-water. Eventually, at Takoradi, where there was a small natural bay and headland giving some protection to ships, a large new harbour was constructed in 1928 (Fig. 13). Takoradi was for some years the largest port in Ghana and the old harbour of Sekondi fell idle.

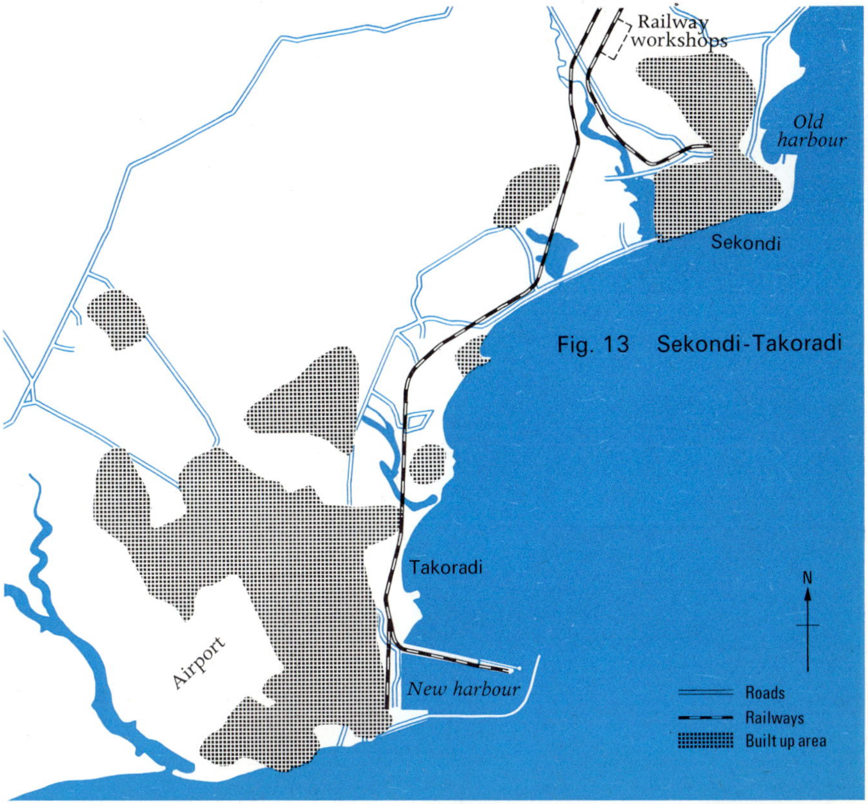

Fig. 13 Sekondi-Takoradi

Photo. 12 The aluminium plant at Tema

Photo. 13 A drowned valley behind the Volta dam. Canoes are used for fishing.

At Accra the surf boats continued to be used, but thirty kilometres away to the east is Tema where in 1954 another large new harbour began construction. This new port is now the largest port in Ghana and is connected to Accra by road and railway. One of the main reasons for building the new harbour at Tema is to provide a port for the bauxite industry in Ghana.

Aluminium is made from bauxite and is one of the most important metals used today. It is very light, and when combined with other metals like copper and zinc it produces strong alloys for aeroplane building. In purer forms, it is a soft metal which can easily and cheaply be formed into pots and pans, or window frames and curtain rails, and unlike steel or iron it will not rust. It is much used, too, in shipbuilding and for the lighter framework of some buildings.

The Volta River Project

In Ghana there are bauxite deposits at Awaso. To reduce bauxite to aluminium requires large amounts of electric power. The waters of the Volta river are used to generate this power. The Ghanaians built a huge dam across the narrow gorge of the Volta. This dam ponded up the river waters

Fig. 14 The Volta River Dam and lake

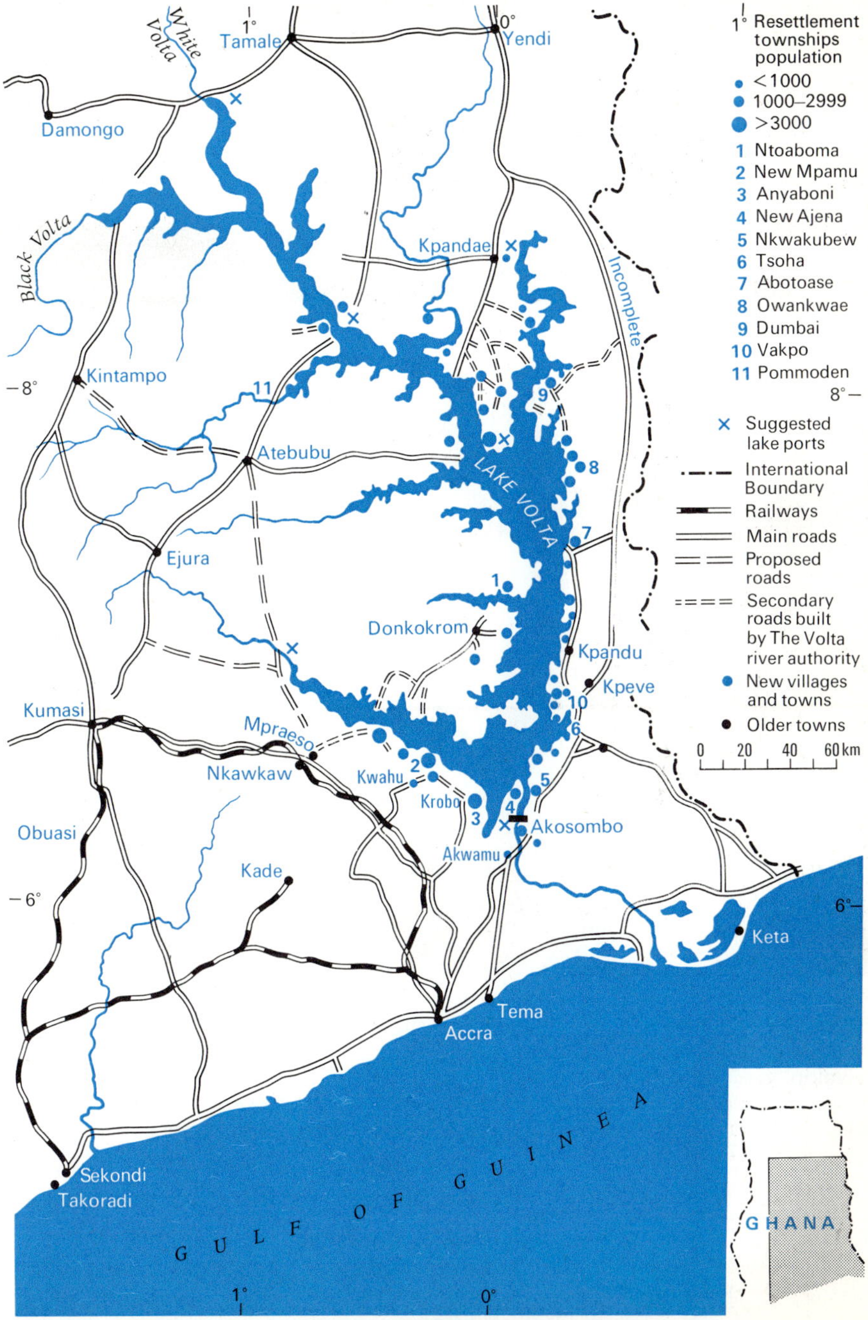

so that they could escape only through tunnels in the dam. The fast, rushing water drives turbines and the spinning shaft of the turbines is geared to drive dynamos to generate electricity.

The power from the generators is taken by overhead wires to a large aluminium refinery at Tema. Extra bauxite is imported from Jamaica and Guyana. The power not absorbed by the aluminium works, about half the total, is being made available for other uses, including electric lights, refrigerators, radios and television, and big new industries will also be started. The Volta project is changing the life of the people of southern Ghana.

Behind the new dam there has formed a great lake. The Volta river valley above Akosombo has been entirely drowned. Many thousands of people used to live in this area; there were 739 villages and small towns. From 1962, when the dam was begun, these people had to be moved. They were asked where they would like to move to. Usually they chose to stay with the same neighbours and move to newly built villages with good farming land near the edges of the new lake. The map (Fig. 14) shows how the new villages and towns are positioned

Photo. 14 Community centre at Tarkwa. There is a concert hall, library and spacious hall for meetings.

Photo. 15 Ghana's electronics industry is developing along with the increased production of electricity.

close to the lake shores. In most cases land had to be cleared of forest before the people could grow their crops. Farmers were shown how to grow new types of crop and the government of Ghana provided some farm machinery, fertilizers, and scientific advice to get things off to a good start.

Things have not always gone quite right with this scheme. Some of the farmers found, when they reached their new village, that the land had not been cleared, and they had to wait a long time for the government machinery to arrive to do the job. Some of the new crops were spoiled by bad weather the first year, and sometimes even when they had a good crop they could find no way of selling it. In spite of the new roads, they were sometimes forced to carry their bundles of tobacco, groundnuts, or corn for many kilometres before reaching any town where there was a market.

Many of the new villagers have taken up fishing. Soon after it formed, the lake began to swarm with fish, and now over 4000 canoes are operating to catch them. Another way in which the lake helps people is by providing a new transport system. The Volta river was too shallow and rocky for ships but the lake is very deep. Two big vessels have started operating. Iron ore from the north of the country and from the eastern borders will be carried by rail to the lake, then by ship to Akosombo, and finally by rail again to a new steel works at Tema.

Ghana is a developing country. The first roads were built only in the later part of the nineteenth century. Now there is a network of roads; there are railways and airfields.

Photo. 16 Gold mining

In the northern parts of the country, however, there are very few mines, no factories or large cities. In many ways, life goes on very much as it used to. During the hungry season in these areas, quite a lot of people decide they will leave their homes and go south. Perhaps they will be able to work in one of the new factories in Accra, or on the dockside at Tema. If they are fortunate, they may be able to send some of their money home to help the family through the hungry time. In the south, new cities are growing. Factories, modern buildings, schools, colleges, a university, and a great new power station—all these things mean wealth in the long run for many of the people of Ghana. But rapid growth brings problems too; farmers were driven out by the waters of the new lake and some of them went to live in Accra.

There are not enough jobs for all the people who have moved into the big cities of Accra and Kumasi. When a father of a family has no land and no job, he cannot provide all that his growing children will need. The government of Ghana has the major task of providing jobs for all its citizens. One of the ways of doing this is to build factories, but to do so costs money.

How can the Ghanaians earn enough to start new industries? The section on cocoa on the next page suggests one way. When you have read the notes about cocoa try to answer the questions below.

What do you think would happen in Ghana if the cocoa crop failed one year? Such a failure might be caused by bad weather or by disease striking the trees.

Do you think the new hydro-electric scheme and the new industries at Tema will help Ghana?

What new jobs have become available in Ghana since the Volta dam was begun? Will all these jobs still be open after all the construction work is finished?

Does everyone in Ghana benefit from new developments? Are any problems caused by the rapid growth of cities in the south?

Photo. 17 Cocoa trees, carrying the growing cocoa pods

Photo. 18 Picking a ripe cocoa pod

Ghana's main cash crop—COCOA

Cocoa trees carry pods on their trunks. When the pods are split open many small beans are found inside. These beans are dried and then may be ground to make cocoa powder and cocoa butter, which are the main ingredients of chocolate.

The first successful cocoa planting in Ghana was in 1879. Although originally from Latin America, cocoa did very well in West Africa and now most of the world's supply of cocoa comes from this region. Ghana alone produces about one third of the total. This varies from year to year according to the weather. Cocoa needs plenty of rain but must be well drained.

The trees are grown in the forest. They do best when they stand in the shade from other trees. Usually a farmer will plant only one or two hectares of forest with cocoa, and he will grow crops such as yams, bananas and plantains among his cocoa trees.

The tree takes five or six years to grow big enough to produce the pods. In the season September to February the first crop is taken by cutting the pods off with a knife. A smaller, second, crop can be obtained in

Photo. 19 Spreading the cocoa beans on mats to dry in the sun

Photo. 20 Inspecting the crop and checking its quality

June and July. The pods are cut open by hand and the beans spread out to dry on mats in the sun in a clearing. The mats are laid on racks above the ground to keep the beans clean. The beans are stirred every so often by hand to ensure that the lower layers dry as well as the top. The dried beans are then put into sacks and loaded onto trucks to go to the railway or direct to the coast for shipment.

Cocoa from Ghana is shipped all over the world, but the chief customers are the U.S.A. which takes about a fifth of the crop, U.S.S.R. about a fifth, West Germany and Holland about one tenth each, and Britain which takes about one twelfth.

The cocoa crop is vital to Ghana. Ghana has few industries of her own as yet. To buy goods such as motor vehicles, clothing and fabrics, oil and petroleum, iron, steel, cement, and the many other manufactured things needed by a modern, developing country, Ghana must sell her own products. She has gold mines, diamond mines, and can also export timber and the ores of important metals like manganese and aluminium. But her sales of cocoa each year are worth more than all these together.

The price of cocoa varies from year to year. But the cost of tractors and other essential imports has risen steadily. How does this affect Ghana?

3 Farming in the Highlands of Kenya

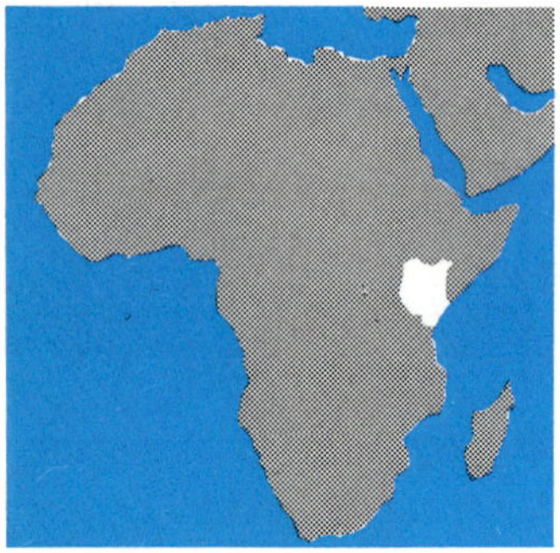

Fig. 15 Africa showing the position of Kenya

The photographs on the following pages illustrate modern farming in Kenya. Kenya in East Africa is an independent country, a member of the British Commonwealth. Turn back to the map of African climates (page 13) and notice that the western parts of Kenya lie in the same savanna zone as northern Ghana. However, this area of Kenya is high land, so even though Kenya lies on the equator the temperature is not so hot. For this reason large areas of highland Kenya were taken over and farmed by British people.

The European farm lands have now been taken back by Africans. Often the large farms of the Europeans were split up into many smaller blocks; in other cases the large estates are now worked by groups of Africans on a co-operative basis. A few European farms remain.

Some of the food crops are eaten by the farmers and their families, but a great deal of the produce is carried by rail or road to Nairobi, the capital city of Kenya. From there, goods for export go to the coast for shipment out of Mombasa.

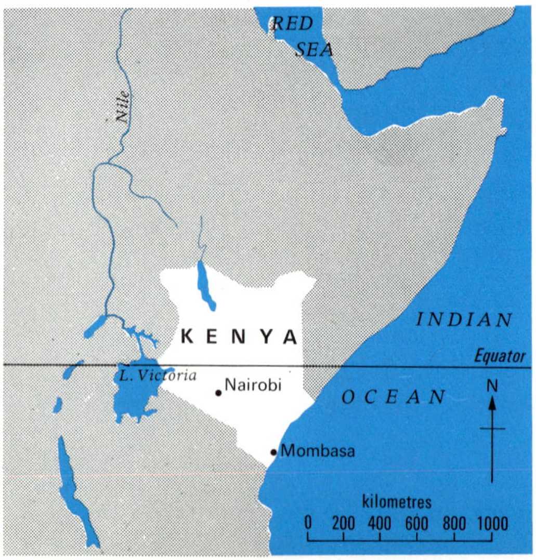

Fig. 16 Map to show the position of Kenya in East Africa

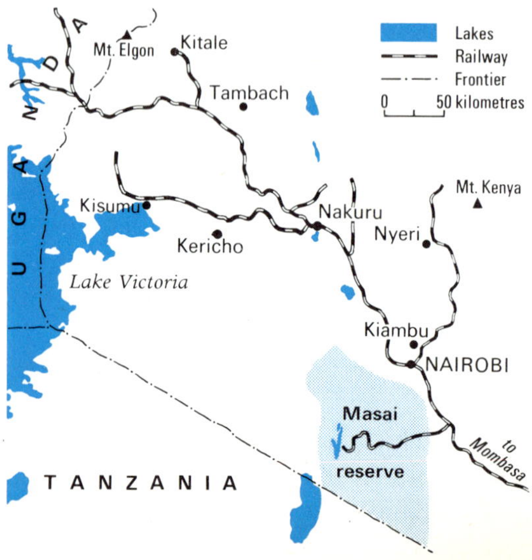

Fig. 17 The main railway lines in Kenya

Photo. 21 Nairobi. The city began to grow when the railway line from the coast reached this area. The railway company chose this as the site for their workshops.

Photo. 22 Centre of Nairobi, the capital city of Kenya

Photo. 23 A wealthy farmer, Arap Tiren, with his family outside their house near Tambach. He keeps pigs and a dairy herd with 'Red Poll' breeding bulls on his 150 acre farm; wheat is harvested with a combine harvester. Mr. Tiren employs about 16 full-time workers, and takes on extra labour at busy times.

Photo. 24 Chief Kipto Arap Chirchir shows one of his fine Corriedale sheep. The chief owns a large farm on which he employs fifteen men. He raises herds of cows and grows pyrethrum and potatoes too.

Photo. 25 Combine harvester on a Kenyan farm. Often such expensive machinery belongs, not to one farmer, but to a group who co-operate to work the land and to market their produce.

Photo. 26 After combine harvesting, the sacks of grain are taken by truck to the co-operative store and stacked there to await transport to Nairobi.

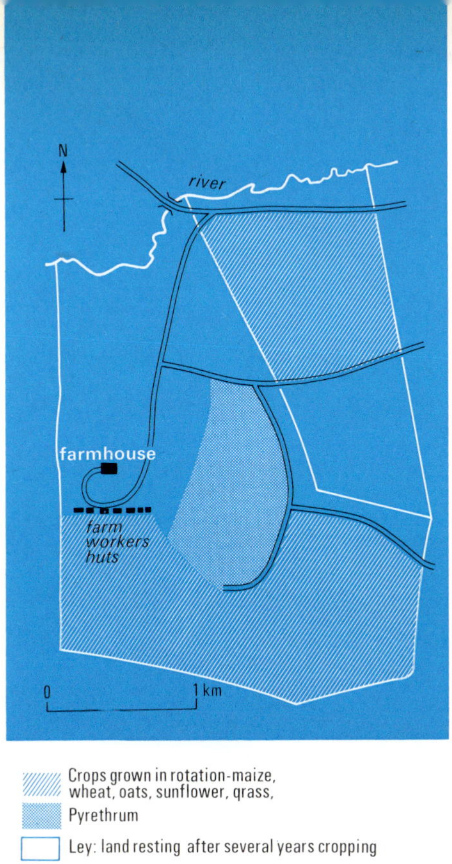

Fig. 18a Plan of a large European style farm in the Mt. Elgon area of Kenya. The farm stands on high ground, nearly 2,000 metres above sea level. The farmer owns three tractors. 70 men work on the land. Many of these live in huts near the farmhouse, and grow maize on small plots near their huts to feed themselves and their families. The farm crops are grown in rotation to avoid taking too much from the soil. There are large numbers of poultry and pigs and herds of sheep and cattle. Farms of this kind have, in recent years, been split up into small holdings and taken over by Africans, or farmed by groups of Africans working co-operatively.

Fig. 18b This farmer has six cows, and sells the milk through the local co-operative. He works the farm with his wife. The bark of the Wattle tree is sold to make a substance used in leather tanning.

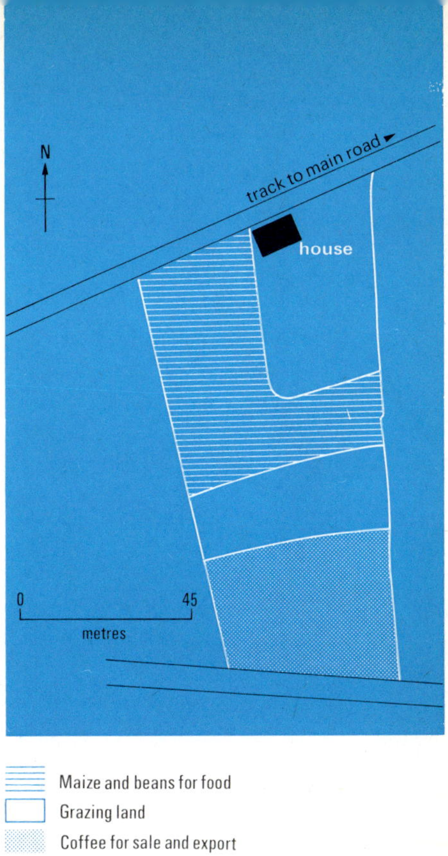

Fig. 18c This small farm is worked by the farmer and his wife alone. The land is 2,500 metres above sea level.

Photos. 28 and 29 Pyrethrum is a kind of daisy. The flowers are picked and spread out on trays to dry in the sun. They are then sacked and carried to the nearest railway. The dried flowers are used to manufacture insecticides. Aerosol fly sprays often contain pyrethrum.

◄ Photo. 27 A hundred years ago, the nomadic Masai tribe pastured their herds of cattle on this land. Now the same land, carefully managed, provides rich grazing for settled herds of dairy cattle.

Photo. 30 Picking tea in Kenya at a height of 2,300 metres

Photo. 31 Weighing tea at the buying centre of a tea factory. The farmer who brought this load in is watching two factory employees checking the weight and recording it.

Photo. 32 Aerial view of a tea factory in the Kericho district of Kenya. The tea bushes are low and closely planted with taller trees to give the crop shade. The round 'pill-box' houses and the rectangular houses with pitched roofs are for the factory workers. The factory buildings are on the right.

Photo. 33 Aerial view of farmlands in the Kericho district. Notice the pattern of roads and the carefully planned village at the crossroads.

Photo. 34 The steep slopes at Kikuyu, an area of highland Kenya, need to be tended carefully to prevent the soil from being washed down into the valleys. The fields are laid out along the slopes to check the rush of water. The village is among the trees on the skyline. In this area, many small, scattered farms have been brought together into a larger unit.

By studying the photographs and maps, and reading the captions, you will be able to make a list of the crops grown and animals kept in the highlands of Kenya.

Compare the farmers and farming methods shown in this chapter with those of the Nangodi in chapter 1.

How would you describe the Kenyan farmers shown here?

Are they better or worse off than the Nangodi? Can you think of reasons for the difference? Has it anything to do with the kind of crops grown?

Does the railway have any influence?

Is it simply a matter of careful thought and planning ahead by the farmers themselves?

Find out what you can, from the school library or any other source, about farming methods in other areas of Africa.

As you study each different area, ask yourself the question: 'What happens to the farm produce in this case—is it nearly all eaten by the farmers themselves, or is it sent away?' For example, the cocoa farmers of Ghana send most of their cocoa crop away (chapter 2), but the Nangodi eat most of their produce, taking only small amounts to market. This is a very important difference.

Photo. 35 Banana trees and a crop of sisal. Sisal leaves provide a strong fibre which is used to manufacture ropes, strong canvas or cloth.

4 Some Cities of Northern India

Calcutta

These photographs were taken in the city of Calcutta. As in all big cities there are modern flats, shops, offices and a great many small workshops and old houses. It is common in India to see craftsmen like tailors and metal workers sitting in the front of their shop, facing the street, working. Skilled craftsmen, shopkeepers, and professional people such as doctors and lawyers live in large houses and often have pleasant gardens. In many ways these parts of the Indian cities are very similar to suburban districts in other parts of the world; only the style of building is different.

Photo. 36 The top picture shows the business centre of Calcutta. On the right is the telephone building and on the left the dome of the General Post Office.

Photo. 37 The street seller on the left is carrying baskets of egg plants (aubergines), beans, chilli peppers and other vegetables which he has brought in to Calcutta from the country by train.

Photo. 38 Around June every year the monsoon season begins. Some days the rain is so heavy that streets are flooded and traffic is brought to a standstill. Notice the balconies. Most houses of more than one storey have balconies where people can sit in the breeze during the hot season.

Photo. 39 Porters in Calcutta carrying goods from delivery trucks to the nearest market. Those who run fastest will transport more loads and so earn more money. Porters are paid by the load.

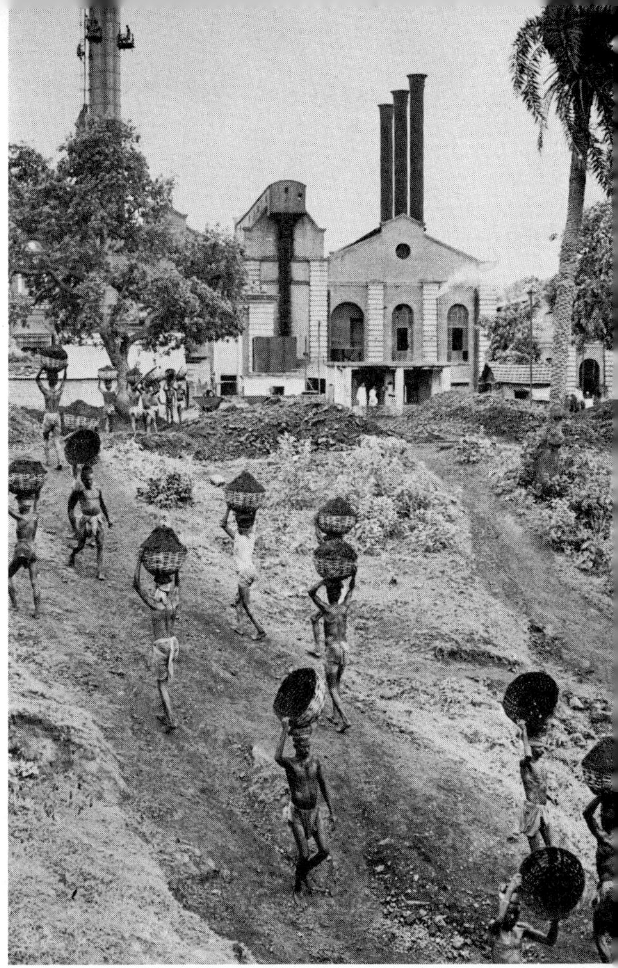

Photo. 42 The Pulta pumping station on the banks of the Hooghly river. A hundred tons of coal are used a day. The coal is delivered by boat and carried by porters.

Photo. 40 Tram car in a street in a poor district of Calcutta. Many Hindus still believe that the cow is sacred, and so the animals are allowed to wander through the streets and lie down at will.

Photo. 41 Traffic jam on the Grand Trunk Road, Calcutta

Photo. 43 This family is homeless. They have nowhere to live but the pavement. During the day time the shopkeeper will open his shutters to carry on business, and the family will have to move.

Photo. 44 These women are drawing water from the taps close by their homes. Their houses are built of brick and are solid protection against the rain. But the rooms are small and crowded.

Fig. 19 Map showing the position of Calcutta in India

In the slum areas, however, people are often crowded into small rooms which must be shared with other families. The rooms may be only about three metres square; any cooking has to be done on the floor. To sleep they must lie on the same floor, no-one can ever be private or alone for long. Probably only one tap, outside in the street, is available for a hundred people; there may be no drains or sewers. If someone living in such quarters is sick it is likely that everyone near him will catch the disease too. Every large Indian city at the present time has areas of this sort.

Measure out a floor space three metres square and then work out what happens if such a room is shared, night and day, by ten or a dozen people.

Photo. 45 Washing cooking utensils in a Calcutta street

	Number of People	Percentage of total	Percentage × 3.6 for Pie-graph
London 1951			
No home or room	656	0.01	0.04
Living in 1 room	221 620	3	10.8
Living in 2 rooms	711 089	9	32.4
Living in 3 rooms	1 695 243	21	75.6
Living in 4 rooms	1 781 945	22	79.3
Living in 5 rooms or more	3 630 682	45	162.0
Total population – 8 041 235			
Kanpur 1961			
No home or room	10 682	1	3.6
Living in 1 room	604 000	62	223
Living in 2 rooms	230 142	24	86.4
Living in 3 rooms	67 003	7	25.2
Living in 4 rooms	30 297	3	10.8
Living in 5 or more rooms	31 947	3	10.8
Total population – 971 962			

Fig. 20 Living accommodation in London and Kanpur

How to draw a pie-graph: Multiply the percentage figures given in the middle column of the table by 3.6 to give degrees in the third column of figures.

Draw a circle of any suitable size and draw in one radius vertically upwards from the centre.

Use a protractor to measure each quantity from the third column of the table to give segments of the circle proportionate to the percentage.

Shade the circle segments in different colours and mark what they stand for.

Lucknow

Number of rooms	Percentage	Degrees
1	2	7.2
2	50	180.0
3	24	85.4
4	11	39.6
5 or more	13	46.8
Total	100	360.0

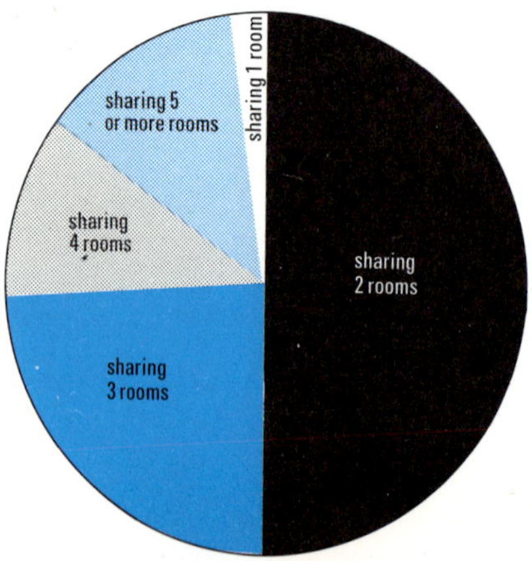

Kanpur

Kanpur, formerly called Cawnpore, is a city of about one million people on the Ganges River in the province of Uttar Pradesh. Its position is shown on the map (Fig. 19). Study the table which gives some facts about living accommodation in Kanpur compared with London. The figures in the centre of the column are percentages, and may be used to construct a block graph or 'pie-graph' showing the proportions of people living in the two cities with good or bad accommodation. A pie-graph is drawn for another city, Lucknow, to show how this exercise can be done.

Note: The situation is much worse than the table shows. Many people in London live in small apartments of one or two rooms by themselves; many married couples without children live in houses of four or five rooms or in small flats. In Kanpur this is almost unknown. Living in one room in Kanpur means sharing that room with as many as eight or nine others. The room itself will be small. In London, there are toilets, bathrooms, kitchenettes etc., which do not count as rooms. Very few people in Kanpur have such amenities. London also has hostels, hospitals, doctors and social

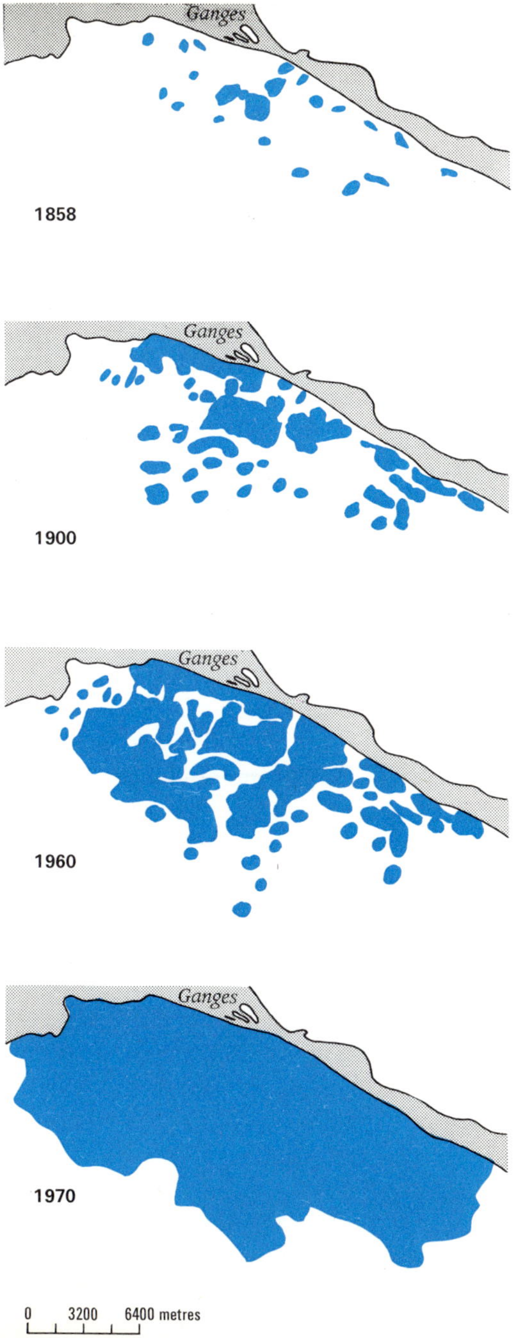

Fig. 21 The growth of Kanpur from 1858 to 1970

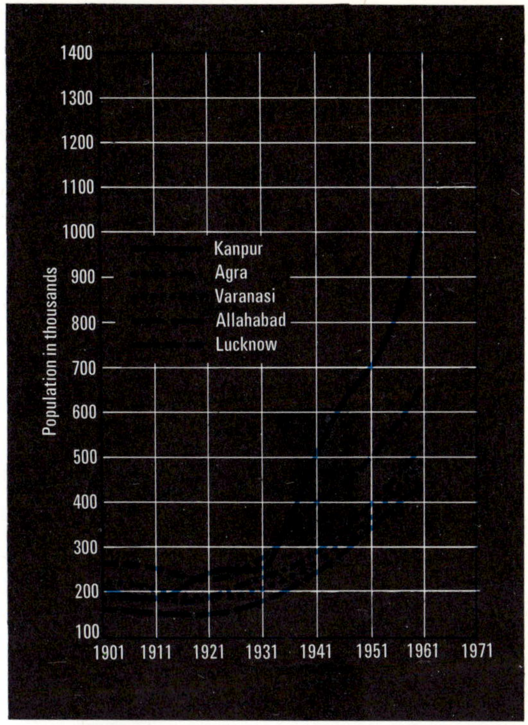

Fig. 22 Graph showing the growth of population of Kanpur and 4 other towns in Uttar Pradesh

workers to help people who are in difficulties. Kanpur has hardly any.

On the other hand, in India at night the temperature is usually high, and in the hotter seasons it is quite usual to sleep outside for greater comfort.

Population increase

Fig. 21 shows how Kanpur grew. These maps show the land covered by buildings at various times. In 1858 Kanpur was rather a small place, but by 1900 the town was quite large. What can you say about the sixty years following 1900? Study also the graph (Fig. 22) showing how the population of the city has grown. Several other cities in Uttar Pradesh are shown for comparison.

Photo. 46 A street in Kanpur. Many of the shop-keepers live above their shops in flats. You can see people standing on the balconies of their homes. Notice the cycle rickshaws which are very common in Indian cities. They are cheaper to hire than taxis.

They are all growing but Kanpur has, since 1931, grown much faster than the others; in 1911 it was the fifth largest; now it is by far the biggest in this part of India. The graph and the map of built-up areas can be combined in a way that helps to explain why so many people in Kanpur are living in the streets or in overcrowded rooms.

In 1900 the number of people in Kanpur was 202 797. The amount of land built up was just over thirteen square kilometres. Dividing 202 797 by 13 it appears that about 15 500 people dwelt in each square kilometre. Some parts of the city were more crowded than others, of course, but it was possible to build a new house with a garden. Some of the newer streets were broad and open. By 1965 the total population had shot up to the million mark while the area occupied by buildings was about forty square kilometres. Dividing a million by 40, the number of people in each square kilometre is over 25 000. Not only has the number of people in the city grown, but the density of population has increased.

From the graph of population, can you make a rough guess as to what the population of Kanpur was in 1971?

What causes a city to grow so rapidly?

There are two causes of growth in Kanpur. One is called natural increase of population. If, every time a baby is born, an old person died, the number of births and deaths in the town (or any town) would be exactly equal. There would be no natural increase or decrease. If, however, possibly because of a sudden epidemic, many more people died one year than there were new births, there would be a natural decrease. It happens that in Kanpur, and in most of

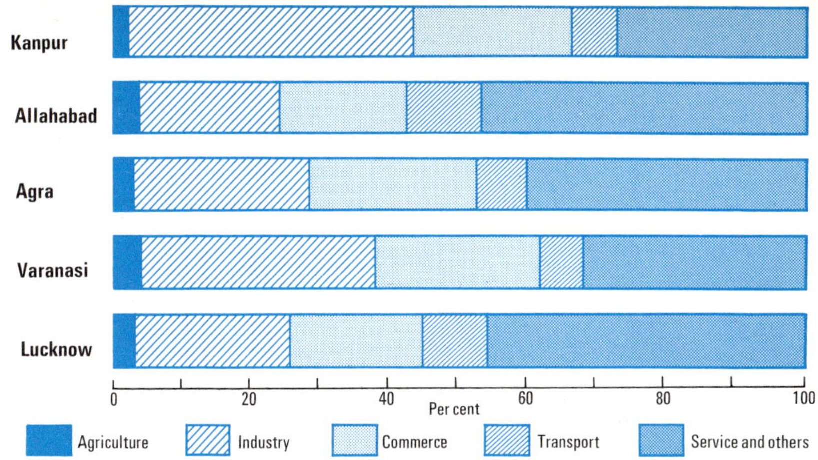

Fig. 23 Bar graphs showing occupations of the people in 5 cities of Uttar Pradesh

India, there are more births every year than deaths. Because of the poor living conditions and the shortage of hospitals, doctors, and nurses, and the diseases that spread through the slums, many young children and babies die, but in spite of these infant deaths, there are still more new births each year than all the deaths put together, so there is natural increase of the population.

Migration to the city

But Kanpur has grown very much faster than can be explained in this way. If you were to question the slum dwellers, you would find most had not been born in the city at all, but had come from somewhere else. This immigration is the second, and most important, cause of Kanpur's growth. It is also the chief cause of the slums.

In the second half of the last century Kanpur became one of the most important industrial cities in India. People began to move into the town to take jobs in the mills, and the population grew. Since 1900, and more since 1920, about 360 more factories of many different kinds have been opened in Kanpur. All needed workers. Some men brought their families with them but many were single.

Nearly all the newcomers were poor people with no money to buy a house or pay for one to be built. Often they could not afford a few coppers' rent required for a room space. Arriving in the town they found nowhere to live except in the shanties and streets; all the rooms were full. New building is going on but as soon as a new tenement block goes up it is filled.

Kanpur is not the only growing city in Uttar Pradesh. Find Lucknow, Allahabad, Varanasi, and Agra on an atlas map of India. Why have these grown? Fig. 23 will help to give the answer. All these cities have large numbers of people in industry; in Allahabad, for instance, there are large printing works, for this is a centre of publishing. But to most Indian people, Allahabad is more important because it is a great religious centre, with many Hindu temples and monasteries and Muslim mosques. There is also a university. Lucknow was a large town in the time of the Mogul em-

Fig. 24 Populations of cities of the Ganges Plain

perors in the sixteenth century and became a princely capital later. It has always been an important government centre and still has many offices, hotels, markets, and a university. These other cities have grown somewhat less than Kanpur, but all are still desperately overcrowded, and all have areas of slums as bad as those in Kanpur. In every case the chief cause is the immigration of people from outside.

Uttar Pradesh is only one province of India. Study Fig. 24. On this map the size of each city of the Ganges plain is shown by a circle of an appropriate size to show the population. In Fig. 25 some of these cities are marked by three columns. The length of the first column shows the increase in the city's population from 1931 to 1941, the second column shows the increase from 1941 to 1951 and the third column from 1951 to 1961.

Which city has the largest increase between 1931 and 1941? By how many people approximately did the population of Cal-

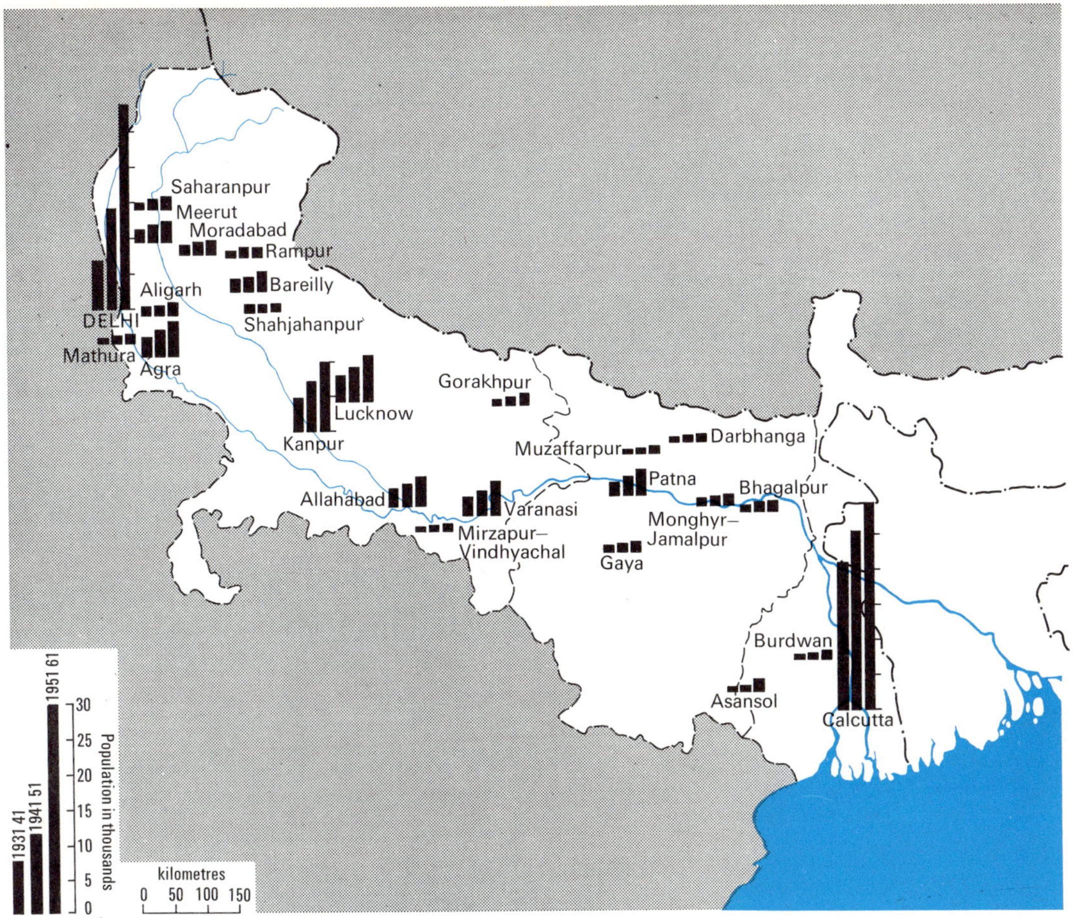

Fig. 25 This map shows the increase of population in each city in thousands for 30 years

cutta increase between 1951 and 1961? What can you say about Delhi during the same ten year period? Are any of the Ganges plain cities getting smaller?

The table on the right gives the population figures of some other important cities in India. Find each city in an atlas and on an outline map of India mark each one. If a city is growing bigger, underline its name on your map in red. If it is growing smaller or not growing at all, write the name without underlining. What do you discover?

Leading Indian cities, population growth 1951–1967

City	Population in 1951	Population in 1967
Bombay	1 839 220	4 902 651
Calcutta	4 578 071	4 764 979
Delhi	1 384 211	2 874 454
Madras	1 416 056	1 927 431
Ahmedabad	793 813	1 414 159
Hyderabad	1 085 722	1 328 164
Bangalore	778 977	1 473 354
Kanpur	705 383	1 139 326

Fig. 26 Calcutta showing improvement schemes

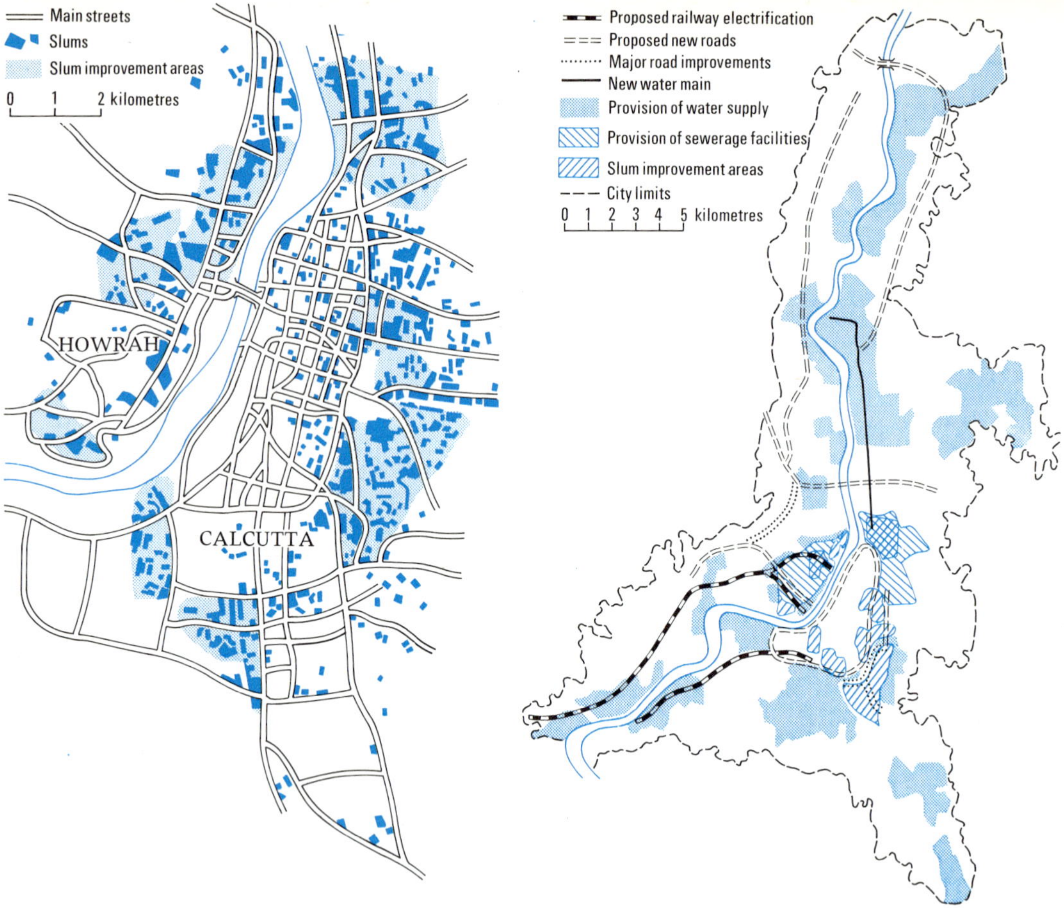

Photo. 47 Though the rains are heavy during the monsoon, there is a shortage of clean drinking water in Calcutta. The government is developing a huge water supply system. Here a new pipeline is being laid. What methods are being used to dig the trench? Can you suggest reasons why so little machinery is used?

City planning

The maps of Calcutta (Fig. 26) show the ways in which the government of India hopes to improve the city. The five year plan includes clearing and rebuilding the worst slums (called 'bustees' in Calcutta), laying new drains and sewers, improving water supplies, roads, and railways. New hospitals and hostels are in the plan, and so are new schools. Diseases such as cholera, T.B., smallpox, and leprosy, may be checked by these and other measures. But one writer who had studied this plan declared 'India is crying for the moon'. The plan has hardly even started to operate. India is a poor country. She lacks not only money but skilled people, engineers, surveyors, architects, planners, and social workers who are needed to put the plan into effect. While the city schools remain as they are, there are very few pupils who ever reach the stage of going to college. As each

Photo. 48 The open brickwork of this block of flats in Chandigarh gives shade from the sun and yet allows air to ventilate the corridors behind.

Photo. 49 New blocks of flats in Jamshedpur, a city in Bihar province

Photo. 50 The central well of a block of flats in Allahabad

Photo. 51 These houses in Jamshedpur, Bihar, have been built in the style of village homes. Families who move into the city from rural areas may prefer these familiar-looking homes to flats.

Photo. 52 Skilled mechanics are building Gnat jet fighter planes.

year passes, the situation in Calcutta gets worse. And Calcutta is one city of many in the same situation.

To see a way out for the Indian cities is very difficult. Perhaps, as well as slum clearance schemes and improvements in the cities, it will be necessary somehow to stop people moving in. In the next chapter we shall find out something about the kind of places these immigrants come from.

Has this chapter caused you to change any of your ideas about wealth and poverty? How do the Indian city street dwellers compare with the Nangodi tribes (chapter 1)?

Supposing you were very poor, would you prefer to live in the country or the city? Discuss this with your friends and teacher. Some of the points you should consider are:
How would you get food:
(a) in the country?
(b) in the city?
Where would you be most likely to obtain shelter?
Where would you stand the best chance of getting a job to earn money?
Where would you be more likely to catch a serious disease?

Photo. 53 These women are carrying the rocks and concrete needed to build a dam. Control of water will help farmers, and also while the dam is being built there is regular work for the people. But in a poor country, who can pay the wages for so many workers? India hopes for help from richer nations.

5 Villages in Bihar, Northern India

Fig. 27 Table showing population densities

	Population	Approximate land area in square kilometres	Number of people per square kilometre
England and Wales	46 017 000	151 000	326
Bihar (India)	46 455 000	173 000	267
Uttar Pradesh (India)	73 746 000	294 000	250
Madras (India)	33 686 000	113 000	298
United States of America	189 417 000	935 000	202
Canada	20 441 000	1 000 000	20
Australia	11 751 000	769 000	15
Belgium	9 290 000	30 000	310

The map below shows a comparison of England and Wales with the Indian State of Bihar.

Use an atlas or school map to find Bihar in India. Draw a sketch map to show where the state lies in relation to Calcutta, Delhi and the cities of Uttar Pradesh. Measure the distances to Calcutta and Delhi and mark them on your map.

Bihar is larger in area than England and Wales, although the two are of very different shapes. The total land area of Bihar is

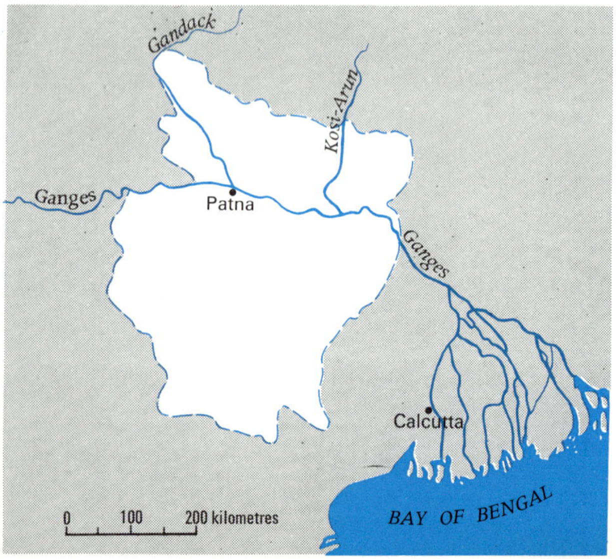

Fig. 28a Cities with over 400,000 people in England and Wales

Fig. 28b Cities with over 400,000 people in Bihar

173 400 square kilometres; that of England and Wales is 151 000 square kilometres. Bihar is about 9 per cent bigger. But at the census of 1961, the populations of these two states were very nearly the same—Bihar had about 46½ million, and England and Wales had just over 46 million. By dividing the total population by the number of square kilometres in each case, we can work out the density of population over the whole country.

For England and Wales (approx. figures)
46 071 604 ÷ 151 000 = 326 people per square kilometre of land.

For Bihar
46 455 610 ÷ 173 400 = 267 people per square kilometre of land.

Generally the state of Bihar is less crowded than England and Wales. The over-all density of population is less.

Compare population densities in the areas for which figures are given in the table (Fig. 27).

The density of population of a country or state is important, but such figures do not tell us about variations within the country. In England and Wales there are some quite large areas, like the Welsh Highlands and the Pennines, where very few people live.

Fig. 29 Density of rural population in Bihar, 1951

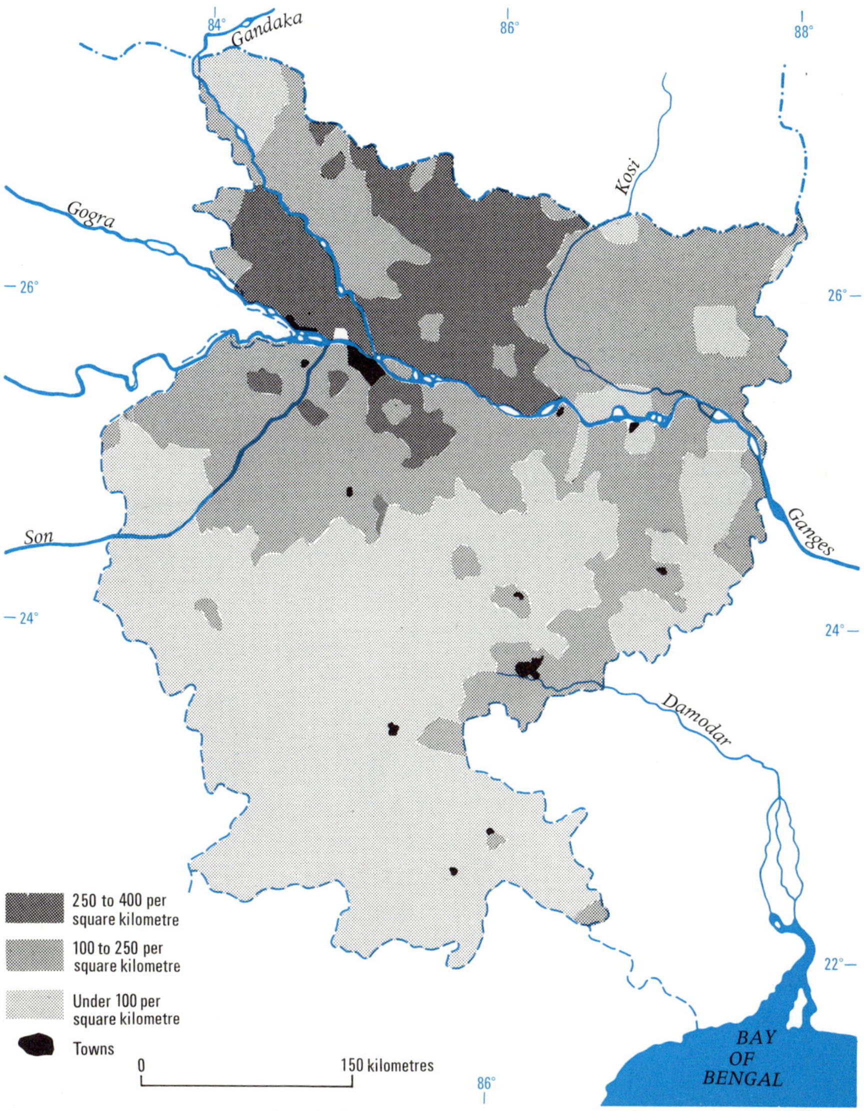

Fig. 30 Relief of Bihar

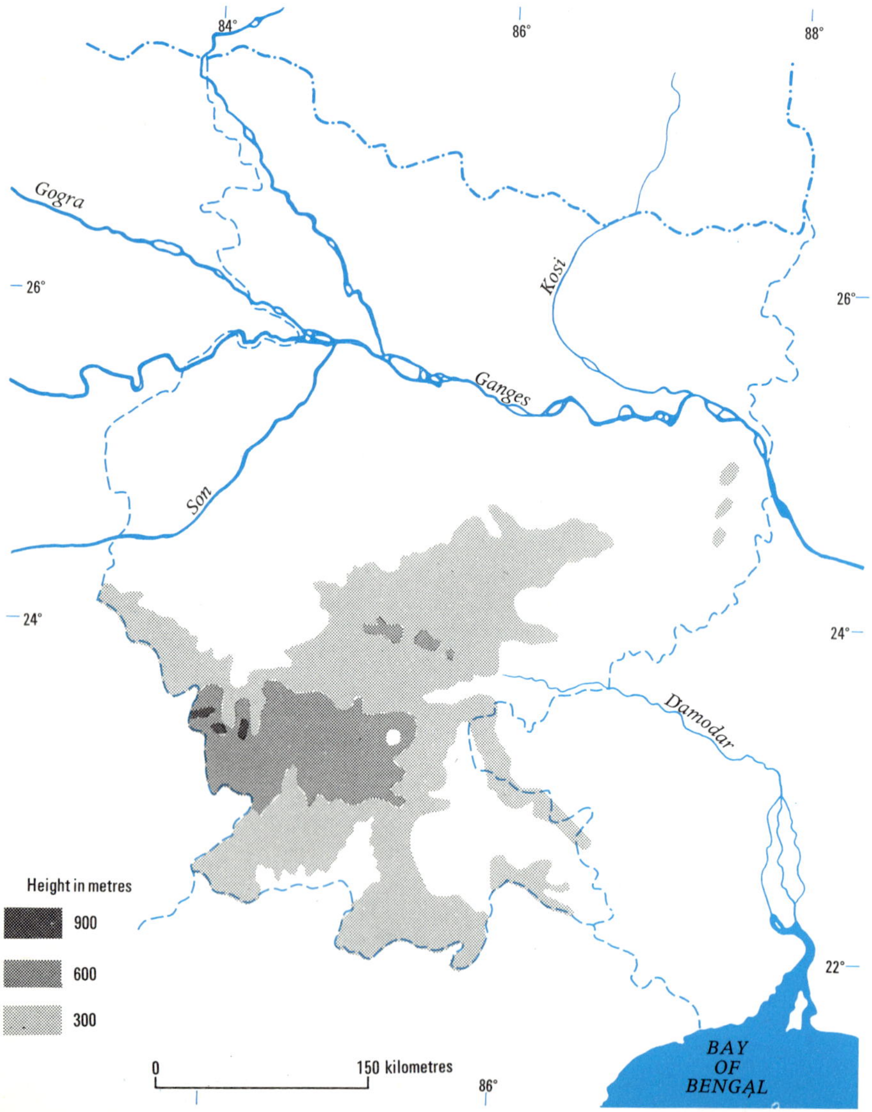

The map on the page before (Fig. 29) shows how population density varies from place to place in Bihar. The areas shaded black on this map are towns. Some of these towns also appeared on a map in the previous chapter (Fig. 24). The largest town in Bihar is Patna, which had, in 1967, 414 506 people—less than half a million. On the map (Fig. 29) Patna is shown in black and it was also marked with a round dot on the previous map (Fig. 28). Each dot on the England and Wales map marks a city which is larger than Patna. How many such cities are shown?

We can summarize what we have discovered so far:

Bihar has a larger area than England and Wales, but has about the same total population. The density of population is less in Bihar. But there are many more large cities in England and Wales than in Bihar.

The tables show the difference between the two areas in another way. Bihar is almost entirely a rural province; only about one person out of every ten lives in a town. There are many millions of people in Calcutta, Bombay, Delhi, and so on. But even so, the population of India is mainly rural.

Urban population means people living in towns; rural population means people living in villages and on farms etc.

England and Wales (1961)

			Pie-graph
Urban population	36 838 442	80.0%	288°
Rural population	9 233 162	20.0%	72°

Bihar (1961)

Urban population	3 913 920	8.4%	30°
Rural population	42 541 690	91.6%	330°

India (1967)
Population 438 774 729

Urban population	78 929 755	18%	64.8°
Rural population	359 844 974	82%	295.2°

Fig. 31 Population tables

Make three pie-graphs to show the proportions of urban and rural population in England and Wales, in Bihar and in India as a whole. (See page 46.)

As the population density map of Bihar shows, some parts of the state are less crowded than others. Use a piece of tracing paper to make a map of Bihar showing the least crowded areas. These have fewer than 100 people per square kilometre. Then lay this tracing over the relief map of Bihar (Fig. 30). What do you notice?

Your tracing of population may be placed over the map of forest areas (Fig. 32). Is this forest area crowded or not?

Fig. 32 Forested areas of Bihar

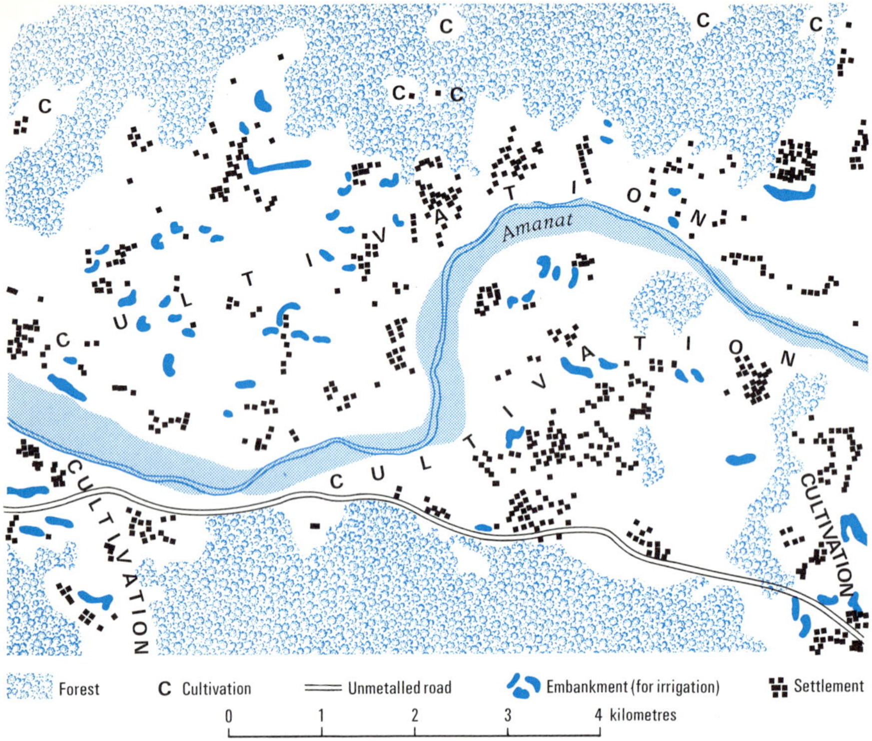

Fig. 33 Settlements in the forests of part of Bihar

Rainfall

Fig. 33 shows a small part of the high, forested land. On this map several villages are shown as clusters of black squares; each square represents a house. There are also many houses scattered about away from the main villages. The forested areas are shaded. Are there any houses marked in the forested areas? Are any houses marked right on the river banks?

The map shows a single, unmetalled road (unmetalled means the roads have no hard surface—just gravel or earth). Villagers who wanted to travel from one place to another might use this track, but on the north side of the valley there is no road at all. People have to walk from place to place on foot-paths between the fields and in the forest. There are many embankments—each of these is a small dam built of earth across a hollow in the ground. The dams catch water as it runs down the valley slopes after rain, to form ponds. In India such ponds are called tanks.

Study the map (Fig. 33) carefully to find out something about the rainfall in this part of India which helps to explain why tanks are necessary. Look at the river, which is

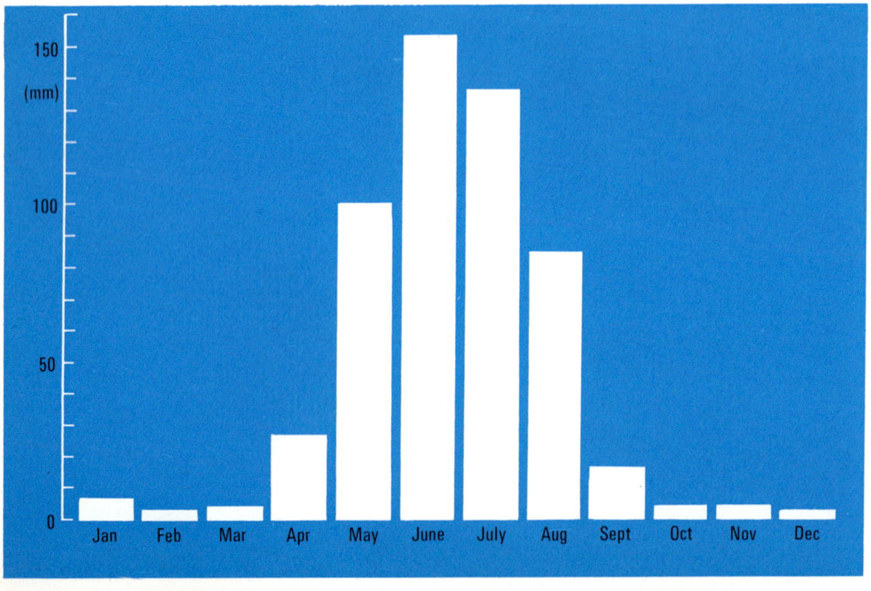

Fig. 34 Graph showing average rainfall of Patna, Bihar

Photo. 54 Irrigating a field in Bihar with a water-wheel driven by buffalo

called the Amanat. Is the river wide or narrow? The map seems to show both a narrow stream and a much bigger one. What this means is that the Amanat is a seasonal river: sometimes a fairly small stream only a few metres wide, often drying up altogether; at other times it is very large, about 400 metres across, with much water even causing flooding. You can probably now say why no houses are built close to the river.

The rainfall graph (Fig. 34) shows that this area has a short rainy season followed by a dry period during the winter. During which months of the year do you think the Amanat River would be at its widest? This is also the time when the village water tanks fill up. This wet season, which affects most of India, is called the Monsoon. The water in the tanks is used by the people in many ways—for drinking, washing, and cooking, but mainly to irrigate the crops, chief of which is rice, often called 'paddy'. Each village needs several tanks.

Before the monsoon, the tanks are dry and water can be got only from the village well, or from the river if it is still flowing. The land is dry and dusty, with a sparse covering of brown shrivelled grass and weeds.

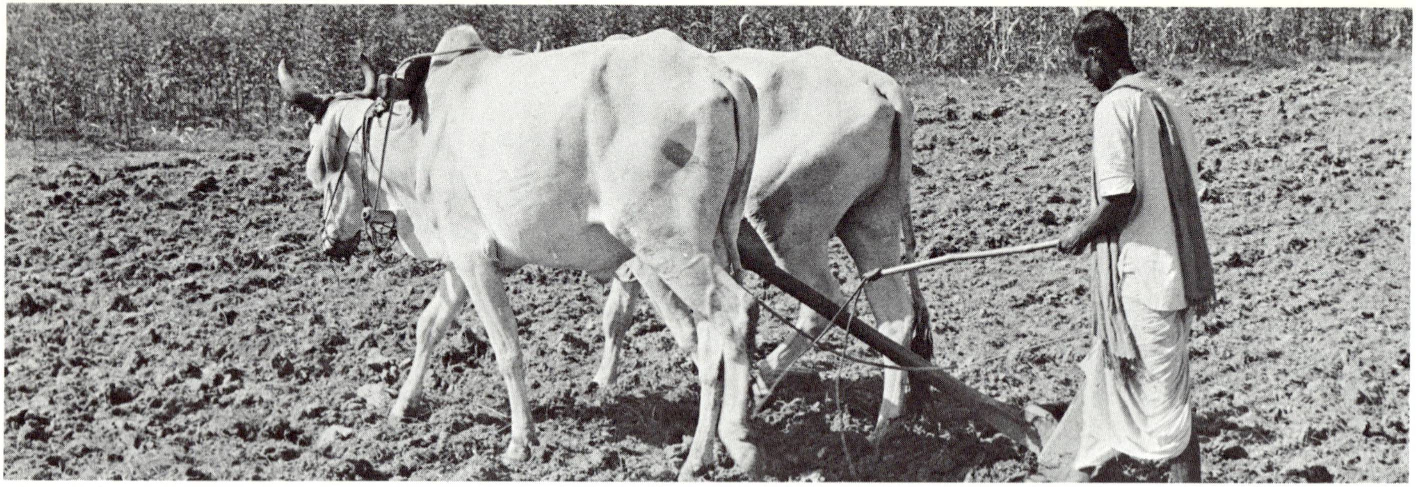

Photo. 55 A plough drawn by buffalo

Photo. 56 Winnowing the chaff from the grain.

Growing Rice in

The fields where the rice will grow are surrounded by small earth banks called 'bunds', and water is let into them to flood them several inches deep. The mud is ploughed while still wet, and the young rice plants are transplanted out from their nursery beds in the best soil. The ploughing is done by a simple wooden plough drawn by a buffalo, as shown in Photo. 55 but the backbreaking job of transplanting is done by hand. In southern Bihar the rice is grown chiefly on the land lower down the slopes below the tanks, because it would be very hard to get enough water into the higher fields nearer the forest edge.

Within a few weeks, after regular watering from the tanks, the rice is green. When the tanks in southern Bihar finally run dry, the soil on the bed of the pond where the water stood is also ploughed and another lot of rice is planted to take advantage of

Photo. 57 A village in Bihar—the stacks are of rice straw.

Southern Bihar

the moisture that remains. Soon, as the rains die away and stop, the rice begins to ripen and the whole village turns out to gather the harvest. The grain is cut by hand with short, curved sickles, and carried to the village threshing floor by bullock cart. The threshing floor is in the open air, and the men beat the sheaves of rice with flails on wooden planks to separate the grains from the straw, and winnow it by throwing it into the air from baskets (Photo. 56). The wind blows the chaff away and the hard grains fall onto the ground to be picked up and husked. The husking is done by the women, with hard mortars and pestles. The husked rice is stored in large earthen jars and is cooked in various ways. The village often has a press where cooking oil is extracted from the oilseeds grown on the land nearby.

Here is a yearly timetable.

Fig. 35 Seasons and stages of rice growing

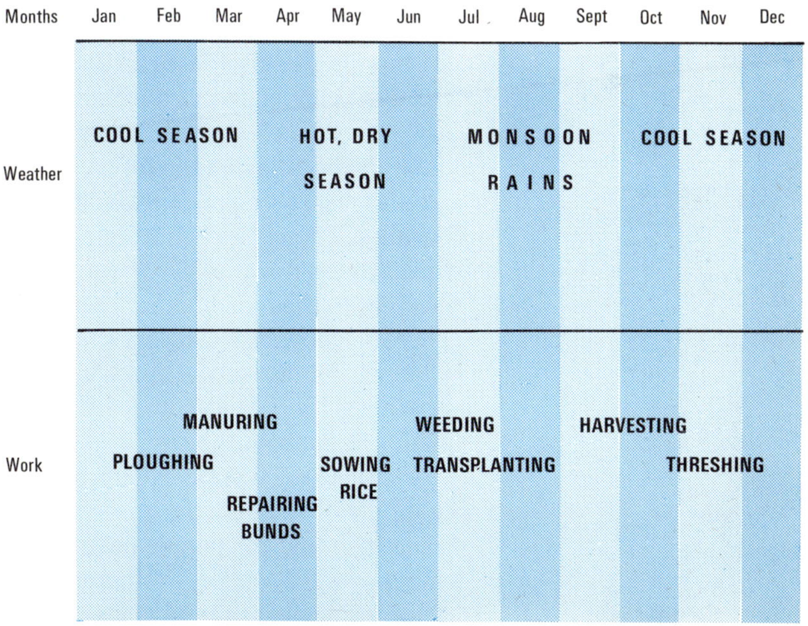

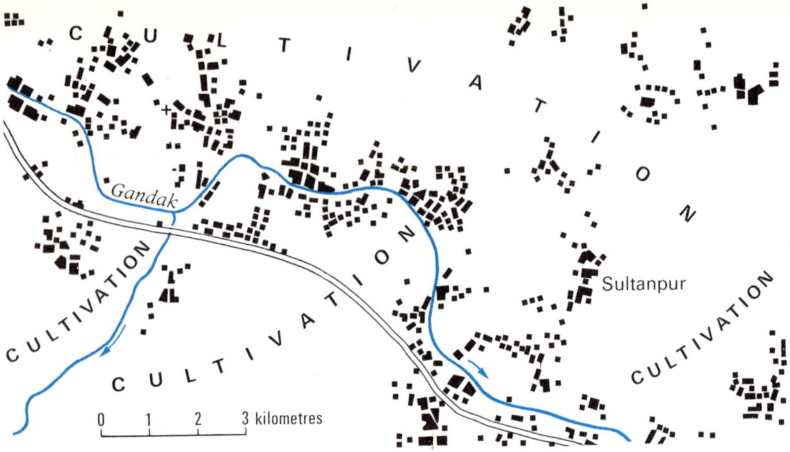

Fig. 36 Levee villages of north Bihar

Clothes and shelter

Clothes are produced in the village on hand looms from raw cotton. Cooking pots and other utensils are made by the village potter, who digs his clay from the river bank.

The people get most of what they need from the land near their home. Even bricks for building a new house can be made from the local clay baked in the sun during the dry season, and timber for the roof and door can be got from the forest on the high ground. The forest also provides wood for burning. The villagers hardly ever need to travel away from home or get something brought to them from other parts of India. There are, however, some small shops in the villages, selling such things as matches, kerosene, tools, and some other factory-made goods from the city.

Such a way of living is called a subsistence economy. Provided the monsoon comes when it should the people have enough to eat; they have shelter, food, and clothing. After the harvest they have many festivals.

Villages on the Plain

Turn again to the population map of Bihar (Fig. 29) and using the same tracing as before mark the areas which have a dense population of 250 to 400 people per square kilometre. (Don't bother about the towns at present.) On the tracing mark also the Ganges (Ganga), the Kosi and Gandak Rivers. Except for a few smaller areas the most densely peopled areas of Bihar are north of the Ganges and west of the Kosi. Laying your tracing over the relief map again, what can you say about the relationship of these areas to the high and low land of Bihar? Nowhere does the land rise above 150 metres. It is a plain. The pattern of villages in this area is shown in Fig. 36 which shows a small area close to the Gandak River.

Compare this map with the earlier one of South Bihar. Is any forest shown? Are there any tanks? What about roads?

All the land, except where houses are built, is cultivated, and again rice is by far the most important crop. There are others, however, like millet, lentils, maize, and sugar cane, mustard, barley, and wheat. The villagers also often grow vegetables and tobacco in small plots near their houses.

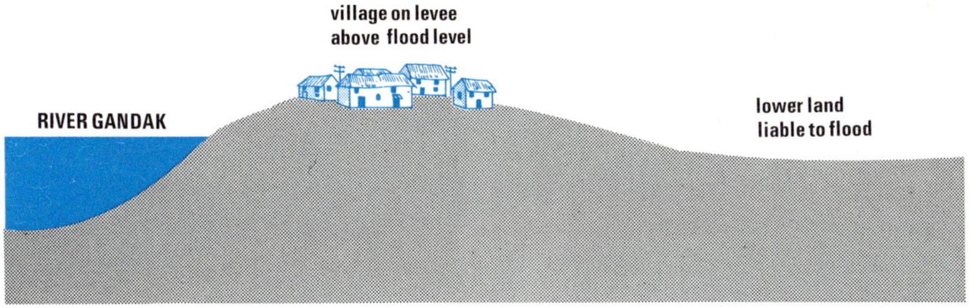

Fig. 37 Diagram showing the position of a levee village

Work on the land is constant. Unlike the people of southern Bihar, the villagers in this area have no period of idleness after the rice harvest. Often there are two rice crops in the year as well as other things to be attended to. The monsoon climate is very similar to that in the south—there is a wet season in late summer followed by a long dry period. Since there are no tanks, the water for the paddy fields has to come either from the river or simply from rain. Usually there is enough rain for the crops, but quite often water is raised from the river by water wheels turned by animal power, or from wells in the villages. The soil below ground is porous, and water fills up the pores to a certain level, called the water table. The wells in the villages need be only a few feet deep to reach water, as long as the water table is high.

Compare the villages of this area with those of the hilly region. They are larger, and many of them are very close to the river. When the Gandak floods, these villages are not swamped by the water. Near to the river the land is slightly higher than further away. In times of flood, the water spreads out over the land from the river channel. Mud, or silt, is left behind. Every time the floods come a little more silt is spread out near the channel. Over a period of many hundreds of years a natural 'levee' is formed (Fig. 37). When people settle in such areas they build their houses and roads on this high ground, and they may even bring extra soil and raise the levee a little higher. Since Bihar has been inhabited for thousands of years, it is hard to say now whether the people or the river have raised the levees most. Further from the river the land is higher so it becomes impossible to get water from the stream to the paddy fields. Crops such as wheat and maize do better than rice in these drier districts.

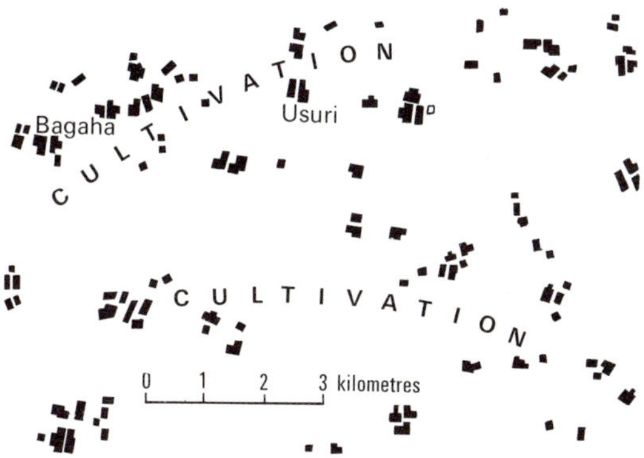

Fig. 38 The villages on the high land are spread out more evenly.

Photo. 58 The Kosi River in the Himalayas

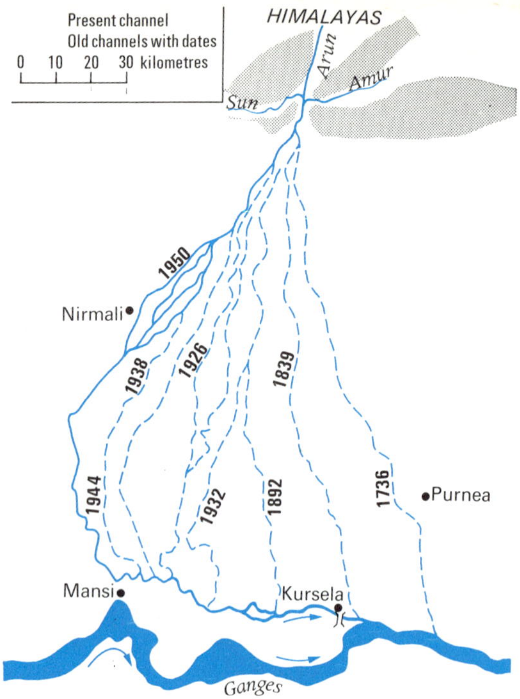

Fig. 39 The changing channel of the Kosi River

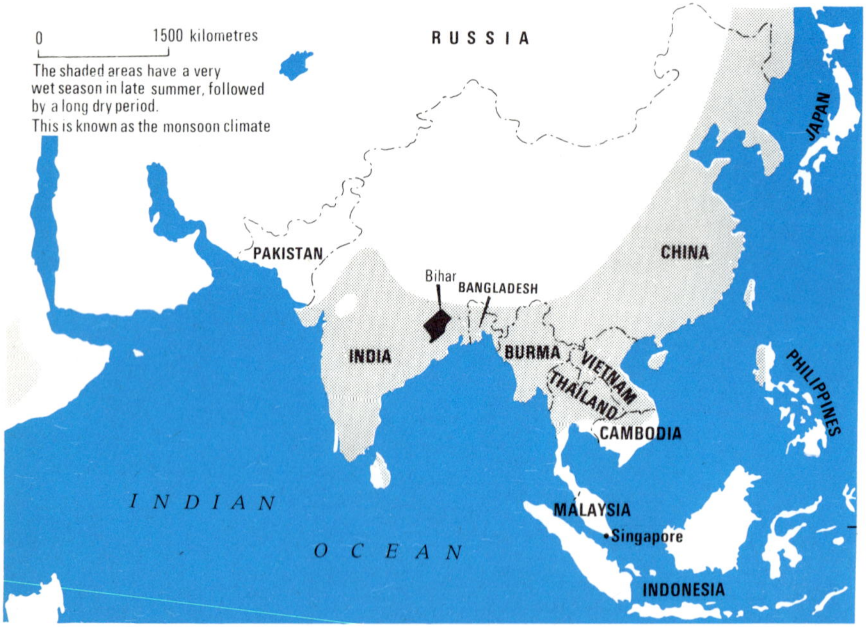

Fig. 40 The monsoon lands of Asia

Floods

If you compare the population density of the areas near the Gandak and Ganges with those near the Kosi River, you will see that the population of the Kosi region is less dense. The reason for this is the Kosi River itself. Whereas the Gandak and the Ganges bring life to Bihar, the Kosi brings death.

The river shifts its channel so that a village that was several kilometres away from the river one year may be swept away by floods the next. Every year the Kosi floods throw about a million people out of work—their homes and fields ruined, without food and shelter, they can only wander away from the areas as refugees. The map (Fig. 39) shows how the Kosi channel has altered.

Photo. 59 Collecting muddy water for drinking from an almost dry river bed in Bihar, January 1968

Drought

The people of Bihar, both those living in the hills and forests of the south and those on the river plains of the north, depend on the monsoon rains. These are very regular, but sometimes the monsoon fails. This happened in 1967. The crops could not grow on the dry, parched soil and in some villages people were very hungry.

Photo. 60 Water buffalo drinks from a muddy pool—all that is left of the village reservoir or 'tank'—April 1966.

Photo. 61 Barren, hard baked mud, Bihar 1967

Fig. 41 How tube wells may bring water when the monsoon fails

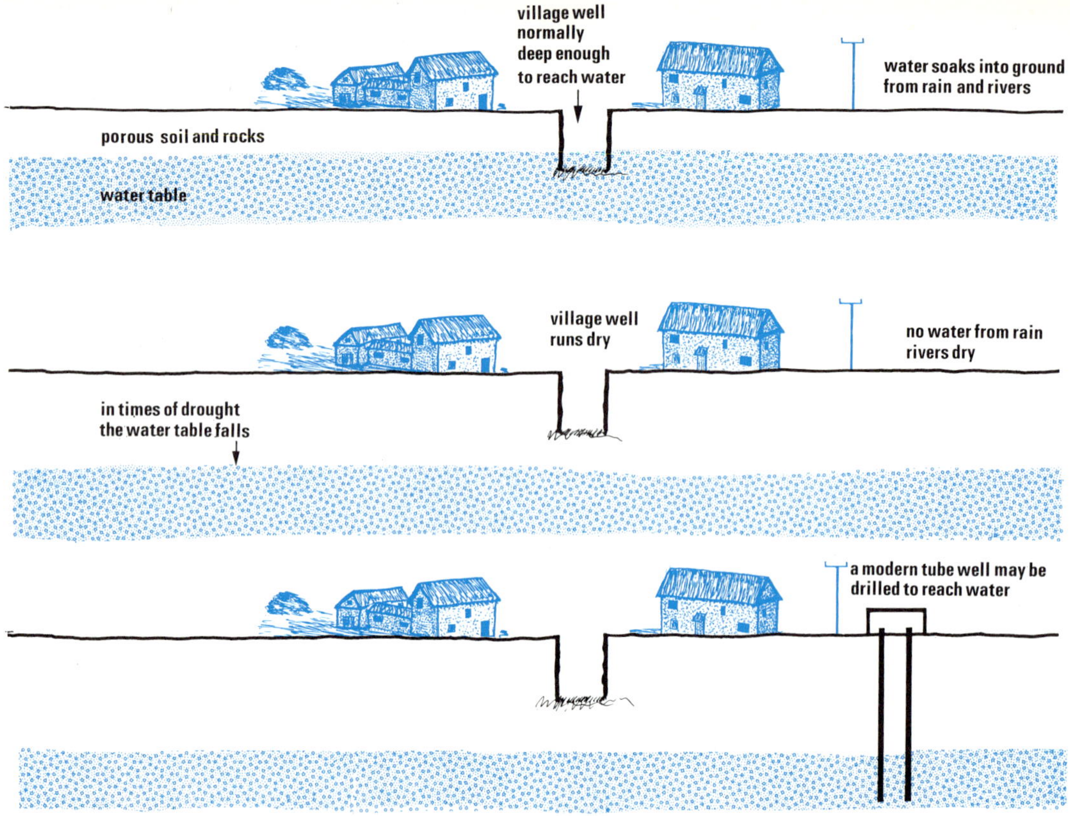

The Indian government has done a great deal to help in Bihar. They have had aid, particularly in drought years, from other countries. In Bihar, in 1966 and 1967, vast amounts of grain were sent to the famine area from the U.S.A., and millions of people who would have starved were saved in this way. But such gifts of food cannot be sent every year, or even every time there is a drought. The answer lies with improving the crops in Bihar itself, and doing whatever is possible to prevent the monsoon failures from causing disaster. Four important developments are taking place.

1 Well drilling

Most Bihar villages have a shallow well, which was dug hundreds of years ago to reach the water table. In dry years the water table falls and the well goes dry (Fig. 41). But with a modern drilling rig, a tube well can be dug down to a depth of several hundred metres if necessary, to reach the water which lies deeper and which is not likely to dry up even after several monsoon failures in successive years. A tube well, as its name suggests, is a steel tube which is sunk into the ground to make a vertical pipe, and the water is then pumped to the

Fig. 42 Growth of the population of Bihar 1911–1971

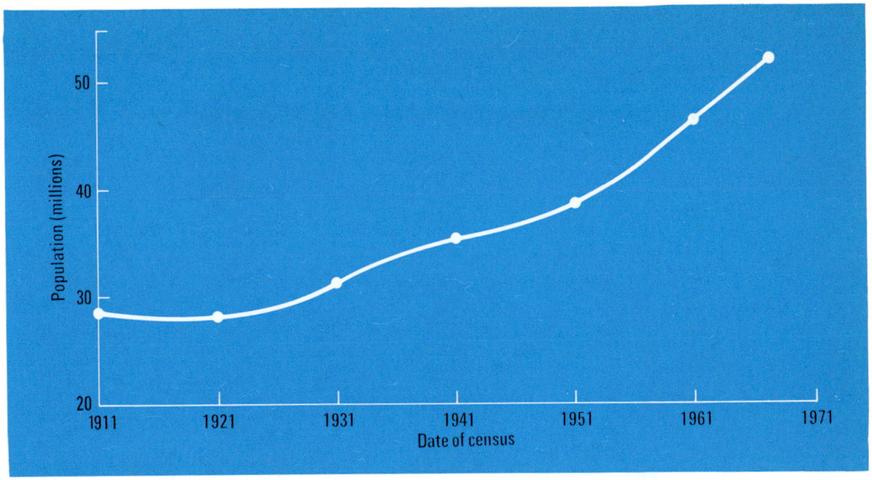

surface. Small pumps driven by diesel or petrol engines are used. A village which has a tube well can be sure of water supply at least for drinking and washing, and some crop irrigation too will be possible. Since the water comes from deep underground, it is clean and this helps check the spread of diseases.

The drilling rigs to make the tube wells, and the pipes, pumps, and motors, are too costly for the villagers themselves to buy. They have been provided by the Indian Government, the drilling apparatus moving round from village to village. Over 300 000 such wells were drilled in 1966–67 alone, and the work is going on still. The supply of water from below is not limitless, but provides a huge reservoir for use in times of need.

2 Training farmers

Even in good years, the village farmers of Bihar and many other regions do not get the best out of their land. They use very little fertilizer and the kind of seed they plant is often not the best, so crops are not very good. If they can be shown how to grow more, they may sell some of their extra crop which would give them money to help through the bad years. This means changing their way of life from subsistence economy (see page 64) to commercial farming—the growing of produce for sale. Such a change would make a very great difference to everyone. The young men who now leave the villages to go to the city slums would probably find more work at home and would be able to earn money there. The extra cash coming in to the village would allow better schools to be built, houses could be improved, the threshing and winnowing of the rice could be done, perhaps by machinery instead of by hand, and so on. To bring about such changes will take a very long time, but India is moving as rapidly as possible in this direction. The government has sent hundreds of small radio sets to the villages, so in the evenings the people can sit in the village meeting place, often under a large tree, and hear broadcasts telling them about new farming methods and warning them of any crop or animal diseases. The women learn new methods of planning their families.

Photo. 62 Letting water into the fields. The buildings in the background house tube wells.

Photo. 63 Tata Iron and Steel Works, Jamshedpur

3 Control of rivers

The Kosi River is at last being brought under control. The huge amounts of water that come down in the floods are now trapped behind a great barrage 1 300 metres long near Hanumannagar in Nepal. The water is stored there for use later on, and the floods are checked. Canals take the stored water down to the farms, where about 600 000 hectares are now under irrigation, growing two or even three crops a year where there used to be only one, and that often swept away by floods. As a result of this new development the Indian Government is hoping that Bihar will, in a few more years, be growing enough food to feed all its own people and have some left for sale to other regions.

4 Industrialization

Improved farming methods in India, the construction of dams, canals, and wells, building new roads and railways, all require machinery, steel, concrete, and many other industrial products. In the past India had to buy these things overseas, but had very little money to pay for them. Now the government has encouraged new industries to develop. A particularly important example is at Jamshedpur (Photo 63). The Tata Iron and Steel works standing by the Subarnarekha River, is the largest in India. It began in 1911 using coal from the Damodar valley coalmines and iron ore from Gurumahisani. Better quality iron ore was later found at Kolhan. Railways now link the works with these sources of raw material, and the steel products, often very large and heavy bars, girders, and rails, go to Calcutta which is 240 kilometres to the east.

Jamshedpur is a new city which has grown up around the steel works in the rather short time since it began. A little village called Sakchi, not very different from the many thousands of other Indian villages, has been replaced by a city of 386 000 people covering over 65 square kilometres. It is not difficult to work out where all these people came from. What would it be like for them to come from their tiny villages in the hills or plains of Bihar to work in a modern steel works? Things were made easier for some of them by the steel company, which built in the city many houses like those in the villages (Photo. 51, page 53). The people could settle down better if they had familiar things to live with at home, even if their work was among roaring furnaces and rolling mills instead of in the quiet paddy fields. In Jamshedpur now it is possible to find these village-like communities tucked away among modern blocks of flats.

Most of the houses and flats in Jamshedpur were built by the steel company and the workers who live in them pay rent direct to the firm. Although the city has grown very rapidly, it has been a carefully planned and thought out growth. The government of India hopes that by building many more large factories of all kinds, the country will become capable of supplying farmers with chemical fertilizers and machinery to increase food production, and that the surplus population who at present crowd into the slums will be able to find work and earn enough money in industry to buy themselves more food and clothing, and pay for better housing.

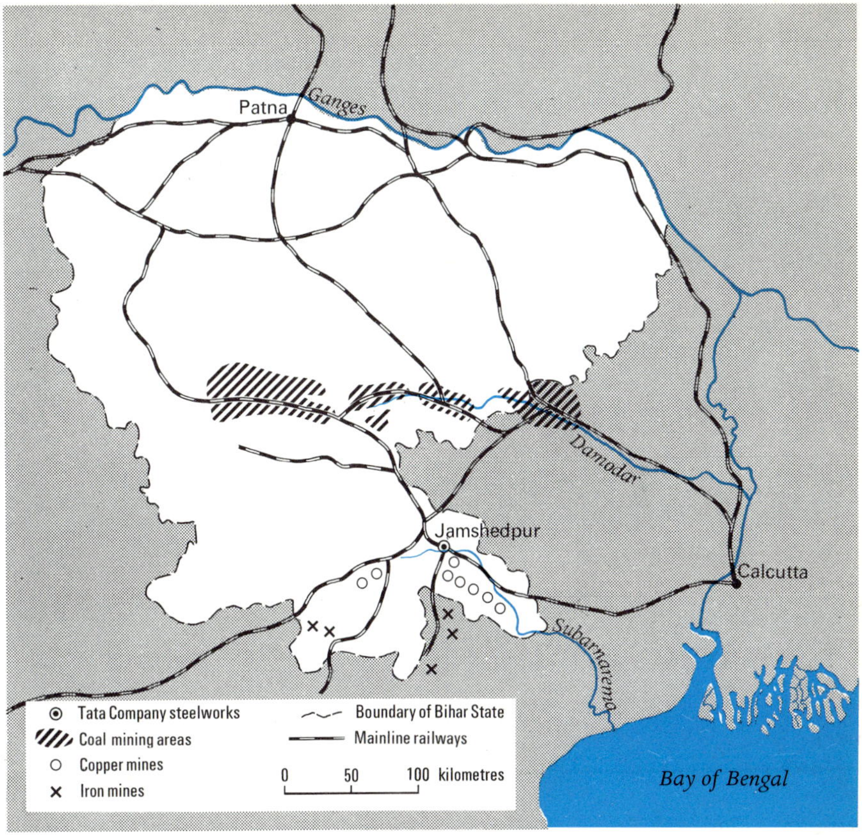

Fig. 43 Industries of southern Bihar

a. Single room dwelling of poorest families

b. Two roomed house with verandah

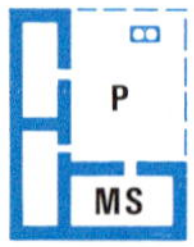

c. L-shaped three-roomed house with courtyard

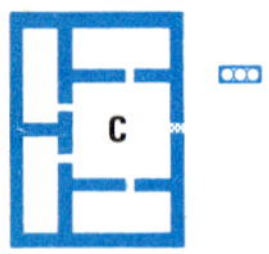

d. Four-roomed house with courtyard

0 10 metres

C Open courtyard
V Covered verandah
P Raised platform
D Deorhi
MS Male sitting room
L Lavatory
K Kitchen
FR Fodder room
CS Cattle shed
Main entrance
Wall
Cattle feeding place
Well
Shade tree

Fig. 44 Plans of houses in Indian villages

Indian villages and

Though India has many very large, growing cities, by far the greatest number of people still live in villages. India has been settled for many thousands of years, and has been invaded many times in history by people who came through the mountain passes in the north-east and north-west. Each new invading tribe or nation brought into India its own customs and religion, but they did not entirely destroy the people who lived there before them. Often the newcomers would settle down in the villages that were there already, but since they came as conquerors they did not mix with the other people and when there was hard, physical work to be done the invaders would make the other villagers do it. Then, at some later time, the land would be invaded again and new settlers would come to the villages, so another group would form. As the centuries passed, there grew up what became known as the caste system. A caste in India is a social group or class. Even far back in Indian history there were castes. They were sometimes of different races—dark and light skinned, tall or short, and so on. These racial differences are still sometimes detectable in Indian society. It was not usually allowed for couples of different castes to marry, and if a person was born into a certain class he would find he was also born into a certain kind of work. If his parents were farmers, he would be a farmer, if they were shopkeepers he must be a shopkeeper, and so on. Sometimes people would break the rules, but not often. The Hindu religion, which is the most important religion in India, allowed castes, and often there were different Hindu festivals and ceremonies for the different castes. For many Indians today the caste system is part of their religion although some Hindu priests do not consider it to be so.

The five main castes, which are found everywhere in India, are:

The Brahmans—scholars and priests
The Kshatriyas—warriors and rulers
The Vaisyas—farmers, merchants, and craftsmen
The Sudras—servants
The Outcastes—often known as untouchables.

However, there are a great many sub-castes and in different areas of India different names are used. In the cities the caste system tends to break down as people move about or take up different jobs, but in the villages it still prevails. The government of India has tried to abolish the 'untouchable' caste. Usually the Brahmans and Kshatriyas are wealthy people who do no work with their hands. In Bihar, for example, strict Brahmans will not even touch a plough, let alone do any work on the farms. They may own the land and take rent from the Vaisyas who do the farming, but give little thought to the improvement of their property. It would be forbidden by the caste rules for a landlord Brahman to sit

the caste system

down to eat a meal with a tenant farmer or for him to touch one of the Outcastes. Certain animals are regarded as polluting and it is forbidden for a Brahman to touch them or have anything to do with them. The cow is sacred to all Hindus, so tanners and leather workers, who handle hides, are polluted by this work. A religious ceremony of purification would be necessary if a Brahman touched a dead cow. Cows are allowed to wander wherever they like, even in the busy streets of the cities among cars and buses. The killing of cattle is not allowed.

In the villages, even today, the castes tend to live apart from each other, and of course the houses they live in differ according to their wealth. The plans illustrate the main types of houses to be found in many Indian villages in western Bihar and Uttar Pradesh.

The smallest houses, occupied by the poorest people of the village, may have only one room for a whole family. This room may be about five or seven metres long but only two or three metres wide. The walls will be of clay, layers being laid one on top of the other, drying out as the building goes on. A thick coat of mud plaster mixed with straw and often with cow dung is spread on the outside of the walls to keep them from the weather, and this coating may be renewed each year, after the monsoon rains are over. In the wetter areas the walls may be made of wattle, which is woven fence-like panels of thin wood strips and sticks coated with mud. The roofs may be either tiled or thatched with reeds, and the rafters project beyond the walls to keep the rain from getting at the clay and softening it.

Such poor houses have no doors, but may have a rough screen which is pulled across the entrance at night. There are no windows. The better houses of the farmers are usually built in the same way, but have often five rooms arranged round a courtyard. One room is a kitchen, another is a sitting room for the men, a place where the head of the family will entertain his visitors. The main door of the house opens into a large room called the deorhi where often the women will sit and talk, or they may sit on the verandah outside, facing the village street. Above the deorhi room there is often a storage space where the family keeps its grain after the harvest, and at night the farm animals may be brought in to the deorhis.

The houses of the more wealthy Brahmans and moneylenders in the village may be bigger, but they usually follow the same general plan, sometimes with two courtyards, one inside and the other at the front of the house surrounded by a wall and outbuildings. There may be a well in the courtyard for the family and these larger houses have lavatories. Most of the villagers have no lavatory in the house at all; there are small pits dug among the bushes on the outskirts of the village. It is very rare for water to be laid on—the supply must come from the well, the tank or the river.

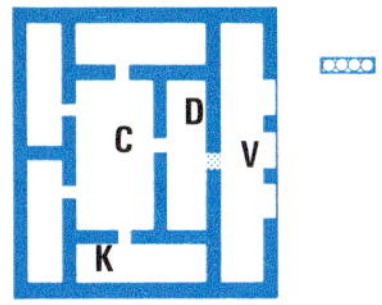

e. Five-roomed house with internal courtyard and covered verandah. The 'deorhi' room (D) is the women's sitting and guest room.

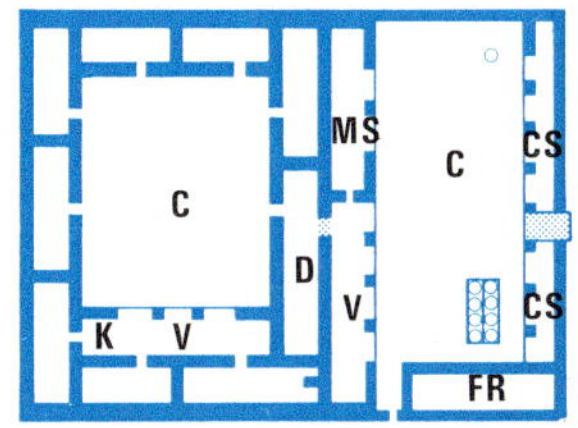

f. Larger house with ten rooms, internal courtyard and cattle sheds around an outer courtyard.

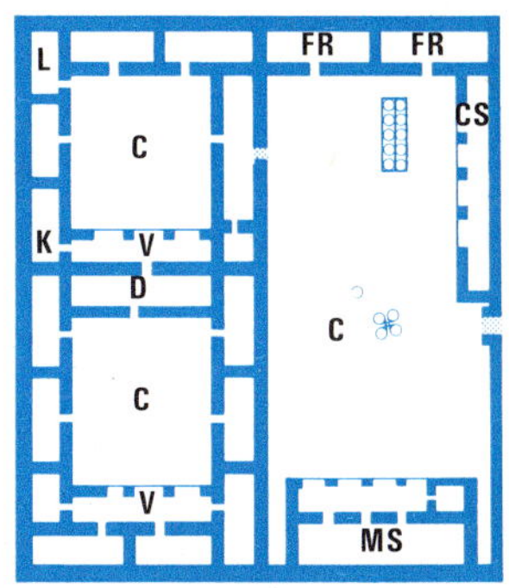

g. A house belonging to a wealthy family.

Fig. 45 Plans of larger houses in Indian villages

Photo. 64 Village street, Perinkulam, Kerala, India

The layout of the village varies a good deal from place to place, but there is always some fairly central open place which may have a larger tree to give shade. This is the village meeting place and whenever important business is to be discussed the people concerned meet there. Nowadays the village radio, usually provided by the government, is set up near the tree in the evenings after work in the fields ends, and the people gather to listen. The houses are grouped according to castes. The map (Fig. 46) shows the village of Aminbhavi in the region of Karnatak near Bombay. The farmers' caste, called here the Lingayats, are the most numerous. The village has a small number of Muslim people, who live in their own quarter, while the large houses of the landlords, the two higher castes, are surrounded by walled gardens. The lower castes, shepherds, servants, and 'untouchables' live on the outskirts of the village. The village has shops, temples, and schools; the positions of the public wells, post office, police station, etc., are shown.

Photo. 65 Street in a village between Tanjori and Kambakonam, Tamil Nadu, India

Fig. 46 The village of Aminbhavi, near Bombay, showing the areas inhabited by different castes

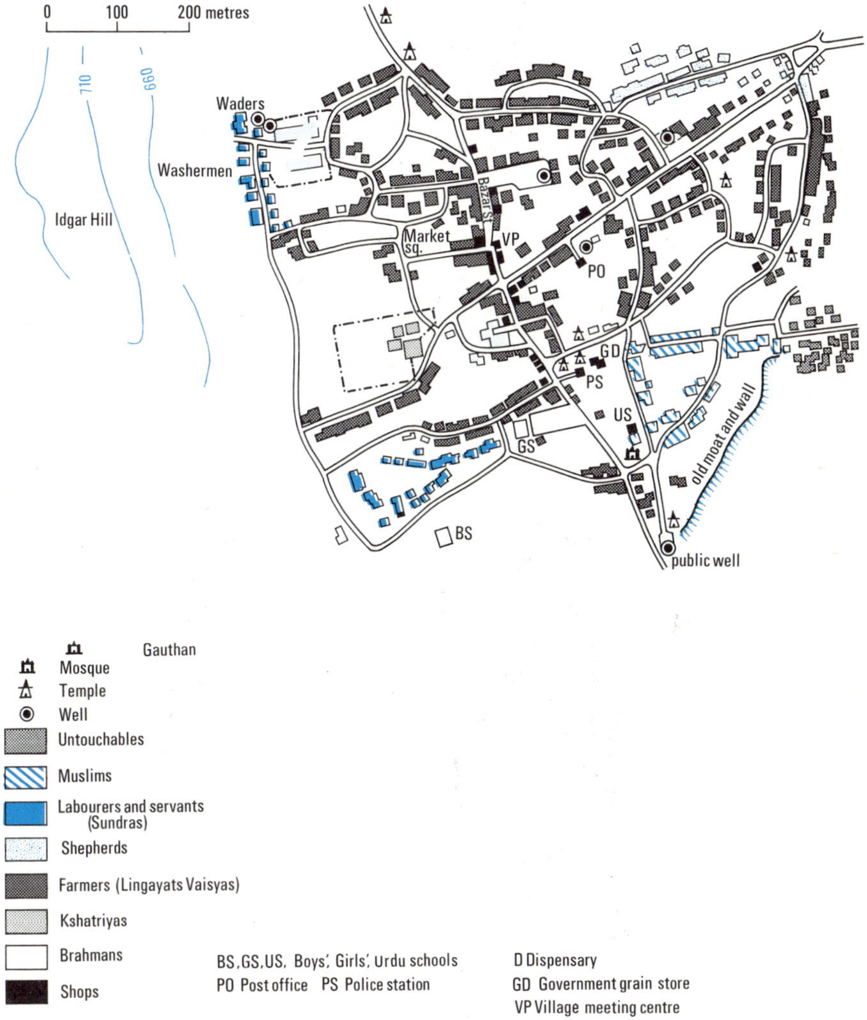

What are the main differences between subsistence economy as described in this chapter, and commercial farming?

Why do you think poverty is less likely if commercial farming is practised?

Study chapter 1 again in conjunction with this chapter on Indian villages. In what ways are the Nangodi different from the Indian villagers, and in what ways are they similar?

Photo. 66 A Singapore street

6 Homes in Singapore

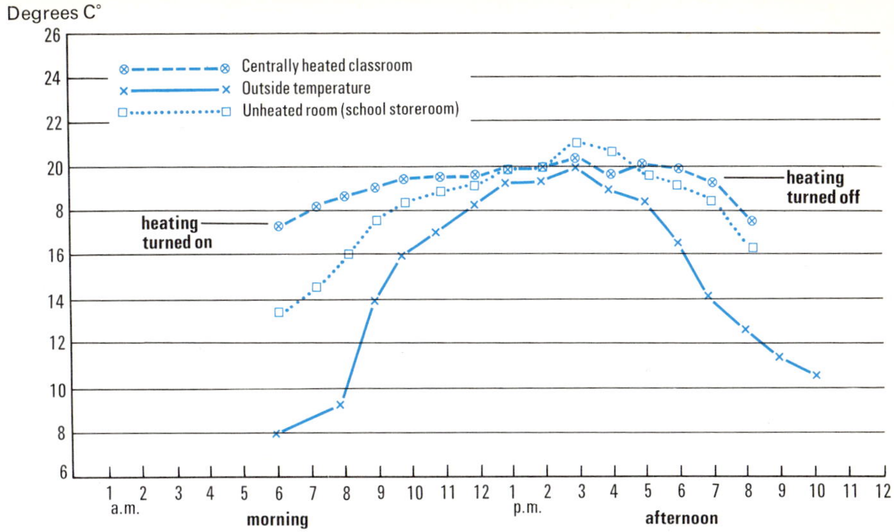

Fig. 47 A temperature chart
Date: 23rd April 1972
Place: Nonsuch Secondary School

Temperatures

What is the temperature of the room where you are now? Find a thermometer and set it up somewhere near the middle of the room, a metre or two above the floor. Leave it for a few minutes to settle down, and then read the temperature in degrees Celsius (centigrade). Is the room heated in any way? There may be radiators, an air-conditioning system or possibly an open fire which will affect the thermometer. If the room is heated or air conditioned, find a room somewhere which is not, and compare the temperatures of the two places. Then take a temperature reading out of doors. The thermometer should be set up in a shaded place, clear of buildings if possible. The best place for the instrument would be inside a proper Stevenson Screen if there is one within reach. If there is no screen available, the thermometer could be hung up under a shady tree or even sheltered with an umbrella. How does the temperature out of doors compare with that inside? What differences are there in degrees?

Take temperature readings over a longish period, in different places. You might be able to take a reading every hour for a whole day. See if you can set up a thermometer at home, in an unheated room perhaps, and read it late at night and as early as possible in the morning, as well as during the day. Some schools have recording thermometers which will register the highest and lowest temperatures reached over a long period, or even draw a continuous line on a paper chart which saves you the trouble of looking at the instrument. If you are able to take readings of this kind, make a chart like the ones shown above (Fig. 47) and mark the temperatures in the manner shown. The example given is an imaginary one. Your own chart, which may be drawn on a large sheet of graph paper, might have to include a lower or higher range of temperatures. You will find that there is quite a lot of difference between north facing and south facing rooms and between those which have large and small windows. Rooms where there is a lot of movement of people, opening and closing doors, etc. will be different from rooms which are left closed up all the time.

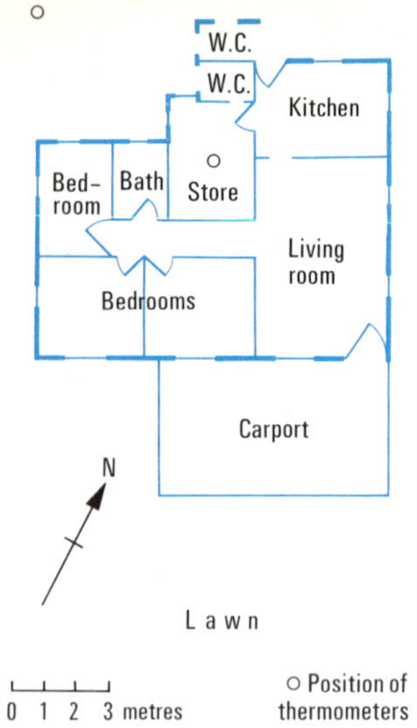

Fig. 48 Plan of bungalow in Tan Sim Boh Road, Singapore

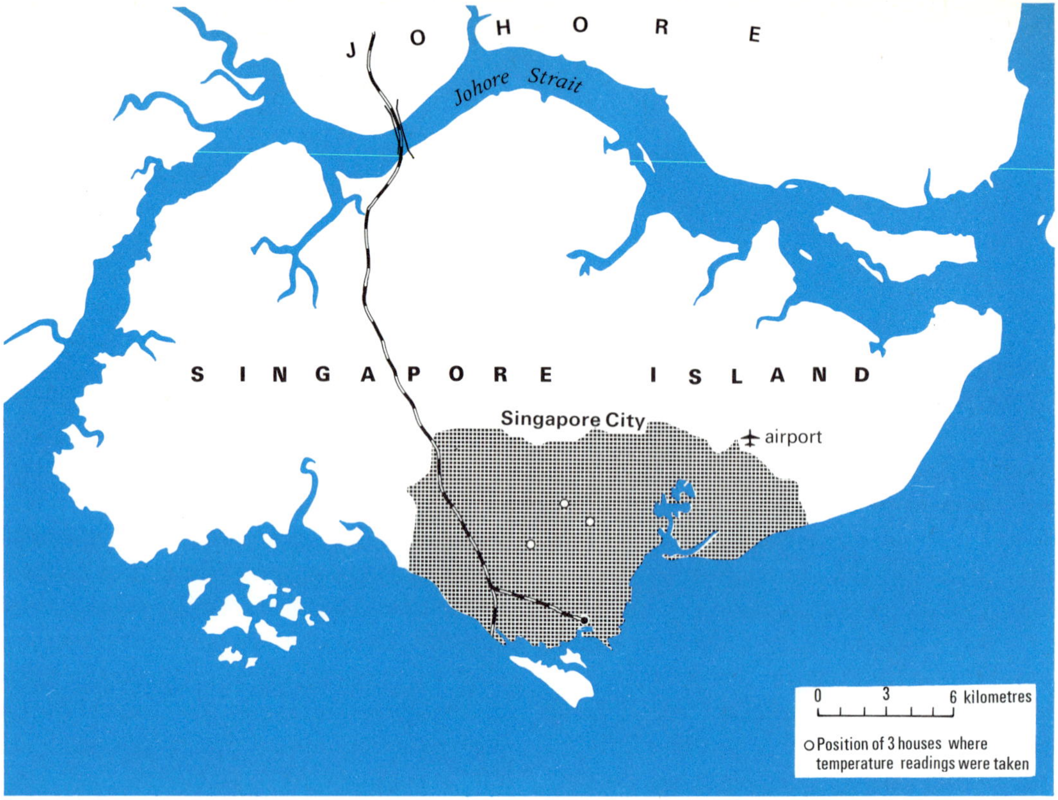

Fig. 49 Map showing the positions in Singapore of the houses where temperature readings were taken

Fig. 50 Temperature chart
Date: June 16th to 20th, 1967
Place: House in Tan Sim Boh Road, Singapore

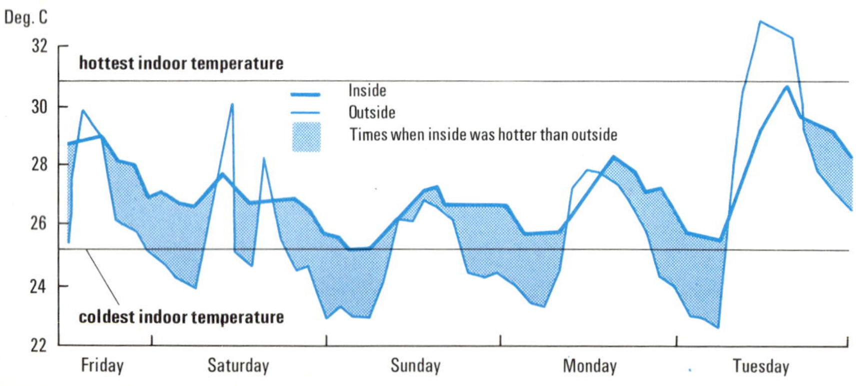

Look at the graph left (Fig. 50). This shows a record of temperatures made at a house in the city of Singapore. A photograph of the house is shown in Photo 67 and the position of Singapore is given on the map above. A plan of the house, showing where the thermometers were set up, is also given (Fig. 48). This house is really not very different from many houses in Britain, Europe, America, or Australia. It is a bungalow with rooms all on one floor, a tiled roof, and a small garden. It stands in an

Photo. 67 Bungalow in Tan Sim Boh Road

estate of similar houses. How does the temperature record inside the house compare with the one you have made? What is the coldest temperature you recorded yourself? What is the coldest temperature in the Singapore house? Compare the higher temperatures in the same manner. Are any of the temperatures you recorded as high as the coldest indoor temperatures measured in the Singapore house? Were your highest indoor temperatures found in heated rooms?

You will notice that no fireplaces are shown on the plan on the Singapore bungalow. There is no chimney on the roof, and the house has no heating plant. The high temperatures are not a result of artificial heating. The outdoor temperatures in Singapore are more variable than those indoors—the nights tend to be cooler, the days sometimes exceed 30 degrees Celsius.

The map (Fig. 51) helps to explain these high temperatures. Singapore lies very close to the equator, where the sun stands high in the sky, almost overhead at mid-day all the year round. Another map (Fig. 40, page 66) shows how Singapore stands in relation to the monsoon areas of South-east Asia. Even the driest month in Singapore usually has more than 150 millimetres of rain. The average temperature also varies very little. In most months throughout the year the outside thermometers read between 20 and 35 degrees Celsius. Notice that even at night the temperature in the house does not fall below 25 degrees Celsius. People accustomed to cooler climates find it very difficult to sleep in such temperatures.

Fig. 51 The position of Singapore

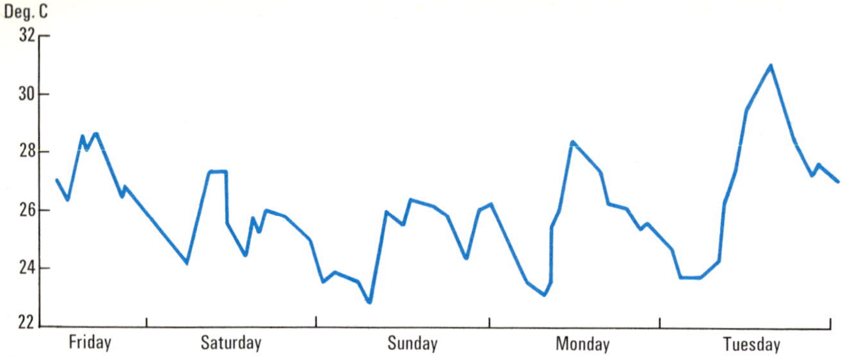

Fig. 52 Temperature chart
Date: June 16th to 20th, 1967
Place: House near Evans Road, Singapore. Make a tracing of this chart and lay it over the chart for the Tan Sim Boh Road house. What do you discover?

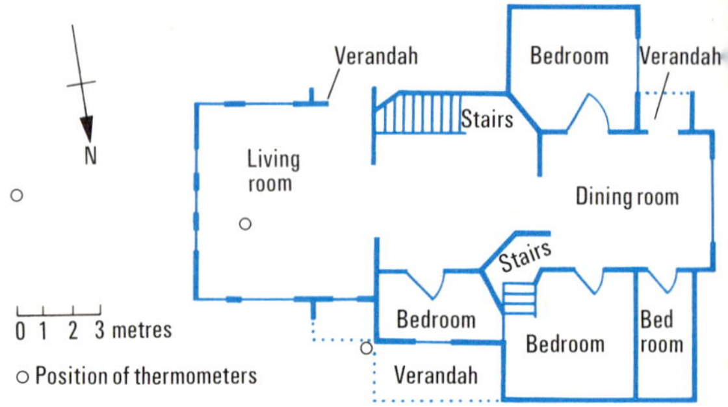

Fig. 53 Plan of the first floor of the house above

Fig. 55 Plan of the house below

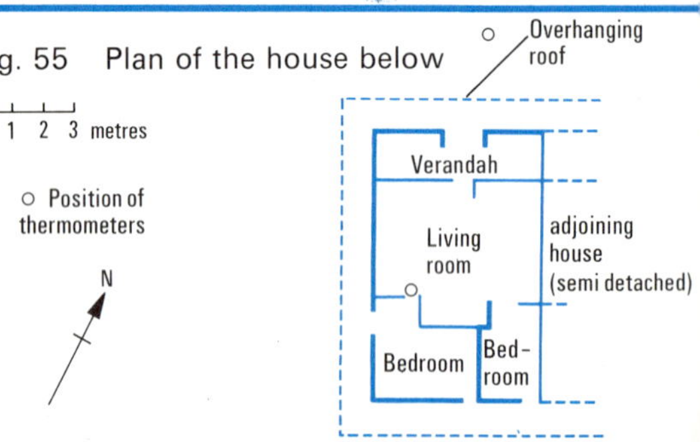

Fig. 54 Temperature chart
Date: June 16th to 20th, 1967
Place: Kampong House, Singapore. Use a tracing of this chart in the same way as you did with the chart in Fig. 52.

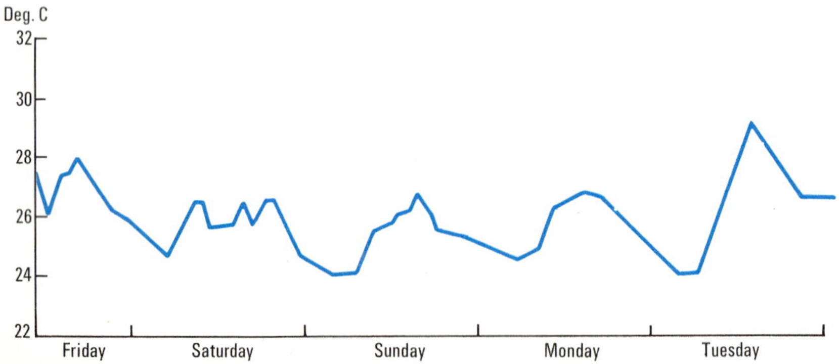

Photo. 69

Photo. 68

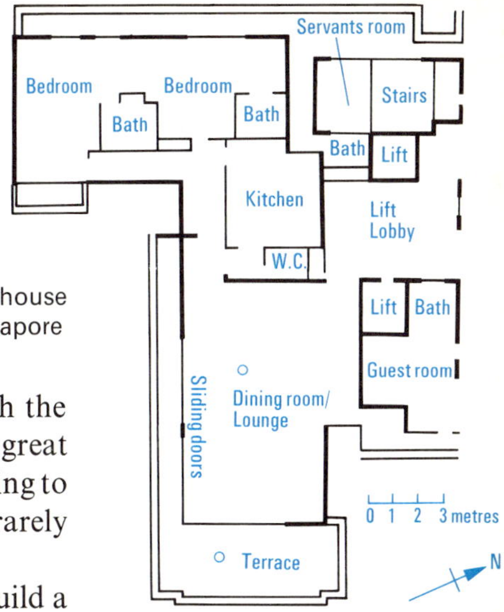

Fig. 56 Plan of a penthouse (top storey) flat in Singapore

Not all the houses in Singapore are like these in Tan Sim Boh Road. That bungalow is built of modern materials—brick, tiles, and concrete. As the day warms up, these substances absorb the heat rather slowly, but when night comes they lose heat slowly too, so that the house remains very warm all through the night.

Photos. 68 and 69 illustrate other types of houses in Singapore. The plans and temperature records of these houses in Singapore are given. The large, old 'colonial' house (Photo. 68) is built of wood with some stone in the foundations. The small 'kampong' house (Photo. 69) is also wooden, with a roof partly of corrugated iron and partly of thatch. Both these houses were built especially for life in Singapore. The Tan Sim Boh house is very like a European home, and in some ways does not seem very suitable for the hot, wet climate.

Compare the temperature graphs of the other two houses. The best way to make this comparison is to make a tracing of each temperature graph and lay them one above the other. With one or two exceptions, both wooden houses are cooler, and pleasanter to live in than the brick tile house.

Notice that the temperatures in the wooden houses fall quite rapidly with the outside temperature. This makes a great deal of difference when people are trying to sleep. Even so, the night-time is rarely cooler than 23°C.

It is of course more expensive to build a house of brick than of timber, but the extra cost does not necessarily mean greater comfort. The old colonial house, as the plan shows, is very large. There are several other rooms on the ground floor, the plan shows the rooms above ground level. The kampong house is very small—there are only three rooms and a verandah, and a very thin partition wall separates the house from the next one, which is exactly the same inside. In Singapore there are some very large blocks of flats as well as houses. Some very wealthy people can afford a flat with four bathrooms and quarters for a servant. Yet the temperature problem remains. In such modern buildings as this, large 'air conditioning' plants are installed. These are designed to cool and dry the air in the building and air ducts conduct it to every room. The cool air enters the rooms through grilles in the wall or ceilings. In this way, the wealthy people of Singapore can ensure a comfortable night's rest.

Photo. 70 City Towers

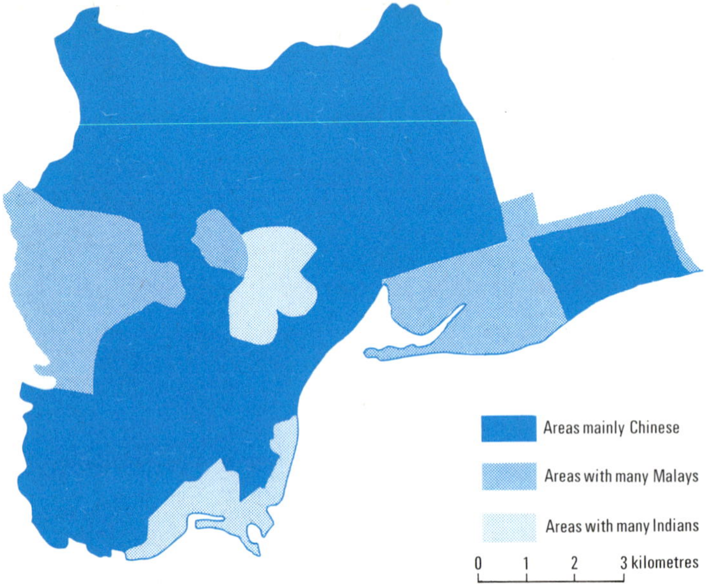

Fig. 57 Area of Singapore

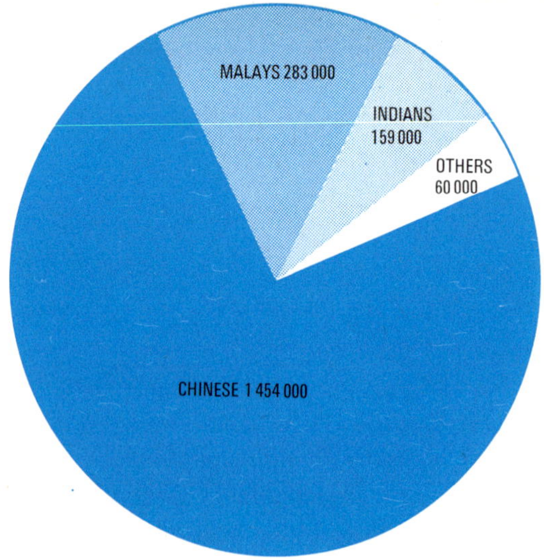

Fig. 58 Composition of the population of Singapore Island

People of Singapore

There are three large groups of people in the city—Chinese, Malays, and Indians. Each group speaks its own language, and has its separate customs and religious practices, so people of the same group tend to live in the same district. Since the Chinese are by far the largest group, they are in the majority everywhere in the city, but there are districts in the centre which are completely Chinese. Study the photographs and discuss the contrasts they show.

In chapter 4 several population graphs for cities in India were given (pages 47 and 51). The rapid growth of these cities by immigration has created many slum areas and in some places people have even had to live in the streets. In Singapore, street dwellers are unknown. Examine the population graph for Singapore. There are two lines on the graph, one for the city itself and the other for the whole island. In 1961 Singapore city could no longer be considered separate from the island as a whole, and the city council was abolished. The graph for the island shows, however, that the total population doubled between 1947 and 1967. How does this compare with the growth of Kanpur in India (Fig. 22, p. 47)?

To cope with the great increase in population, enormous building projects have been carried out in Singapore. The photographs opposite show some of these. In Singapore, the rents charged for flats vary

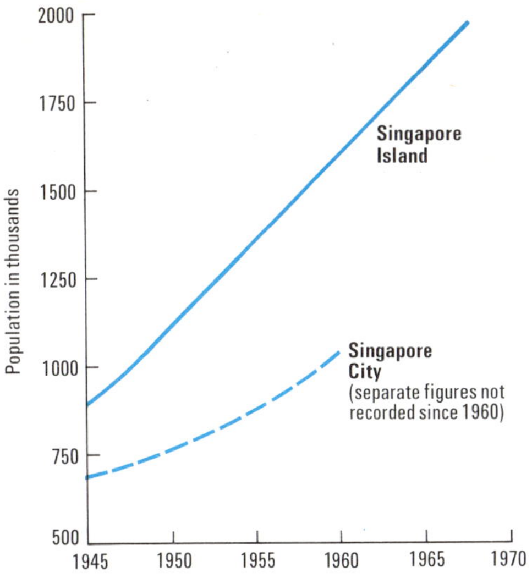

Fig. 59 Growth of population of Singapore

Photo. 71 Modern buildings to house Singapore's growing population—the suburb of Queenstown

Photo. 72 A street of contrasts in Singapore

according to how many rooms there are. A one room flat might cost up to 30 dollars per week to rent (a dollar in Singapore is worth about 3 shillings, so 30 dollars is about £4.50). A flat with two or three rooms costs quite a lot more than this. To pay for such accommodation people must be able to find employment. From the photographs of Singapore, and any other information you can find out about the city, make a list of jobs. Discuss differences between Singapore and Kanpur.

Pig farms in multi-storey flats

By TAN WANG JOO

SINGAPORE, Wednesday

THE days of pig and poultry subsistence farming are numbered. The Government's policy now is to discourage this and encourage intensive, highly mechanised farming.

This could mean rearing pigs and poultry not on land, but in multi-storey buildings.

"The plain fact is that land is just too scare and precious for subsistence farming to continue," said a National Development spokesman today.

"The Government is resettling farmers and acquiring their land for public purposes.

"Concurrently we are working on an agricultural policy to encourage more efficient and sophisticated pig and poultry farming."

The Government, he said, would shortly be coming up with new plans and ideas to implement this new policy.

Fig. 60 This newspaper cutting from the Straits Times of July 22nd, 1971 draws attention to some of the problems facing Singapore.

Singapore is a city on an island. It is an independent state and a member of the British Commonwealth. These photographs show some of the farming land which provides the people in the city with food. The crops grown on these farms include all kinds of vegetables, and because of the continually warm climate it is possible sometimes to grow many crops in one year off the same land. Many of the farms also keep pigs and cattle, and poultry farming for eggs is also very common. Although the farmers often live in quite small, cheaply built houses, they can make quite good incomes from the sale of their produce to the city, and although land is scarce, it has even been possible for Singapore to export some food products to Malaya and other countries.

Photo. 73 A research station for developing new farming techniques

Photo. 74 A market gardener hoeing his land

Are the farmers of Singapore commercial or subsistence farmers? How do they compare with the farmers of Bihar, discussed in chapter 5?

Can you foresee any problems for Singapore's farmlands in view of the growth of the city?

Photo. 75 A poultry farm

Photo. 76 Singapore harbour—pumping rubber aboard a tanker bound for America

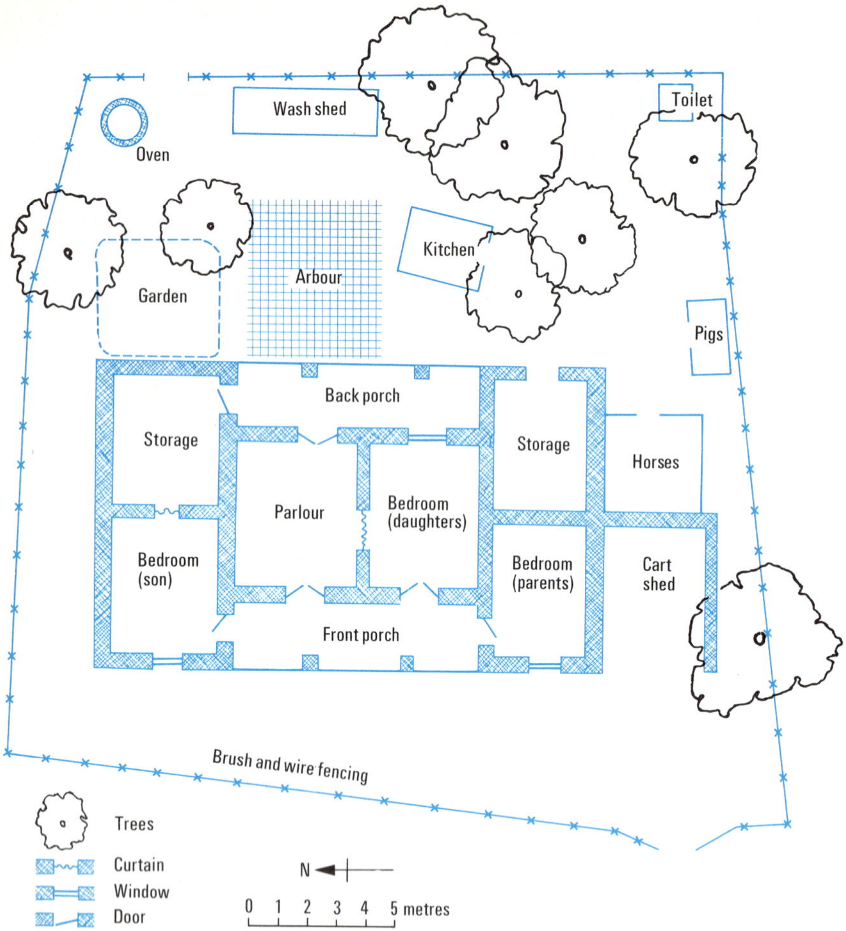

Fig. 61 Plan of a farmstead in central Chile. In this adobe house there are plank floors in the parlour and central bedroom, but no rooms have ceilings. There are only three windows in the entire house, and most rooms are entered directly from the outdoors.

7 Changes in Chilean Farming

The plan on this page (Fig. 61) is of a house in the Cuncumen district of Central Chile in South America. Cuncumen is 90 kilometres west-south-west of Santiago in the region known as the Central Valley of Chile. The building is made of clay mud plastered onto a light framework of thin, woven strips of wood. This kind of construction is called 'adobe' or sometimes 'wattle and daub'. The roof of this particular house is thatched but some others in the district are tiled and even more have roofs of corrugated iron.

There are six rooms, with a front and back porch, and various other sheds and outhouses close to the house. It stands on its own small block of land.

How does this house compare with some of the Indian village houses shown in chapter 5? The graph shown opposite gives the winter and summer temperatures which, in normal seasons, the people of Central Chile expect. The maximum temperatures for each day of January (summer in the southern hemisphere) and July (winter) are given, and the minimum night temperature is also shown. What was the temperature of the hottest January day? Which day of the month was it? What was

Fig. 62 Chart showing daily temperatures for the months of January and July in Santiago, Chile.

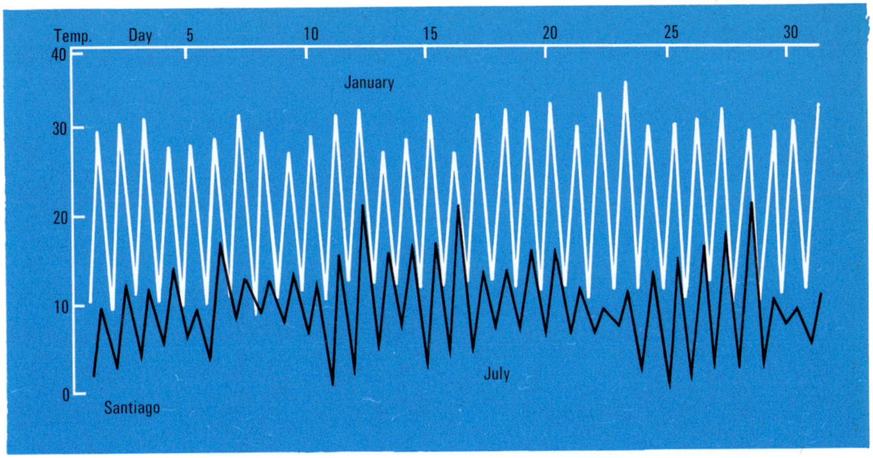

the coolest night of January?

Compare these temperatures with the July graph. What was the temperature of the hottest July day? What was the lowest night figure for that month? What is the *range* of temperatures?

To find this, subtract the minimum temperature of the coldest July night from the maximum of the hottest January day.

The lower graph shows the rainfall expected for each month. What do you notice about this? How does the climate of this area compare with that of the Indian Monsoon regions described in chapter 5?

From the point of view of people living in this region of Chile, which type of roof material do you think would be best? Remember, tiles are waterproof as long as they are laid properly and none of them are cracked. They take some hours to get hot on a summer's day, but once hot they cool slowly also, so the house may remain hot all night.

Thatch has to be well looked after if it is to be waterproof, but it is a good insulator—that is, it keeps out the heat well in summer and keeps warmth inside the house in winter. It can catch fire very easily, however.

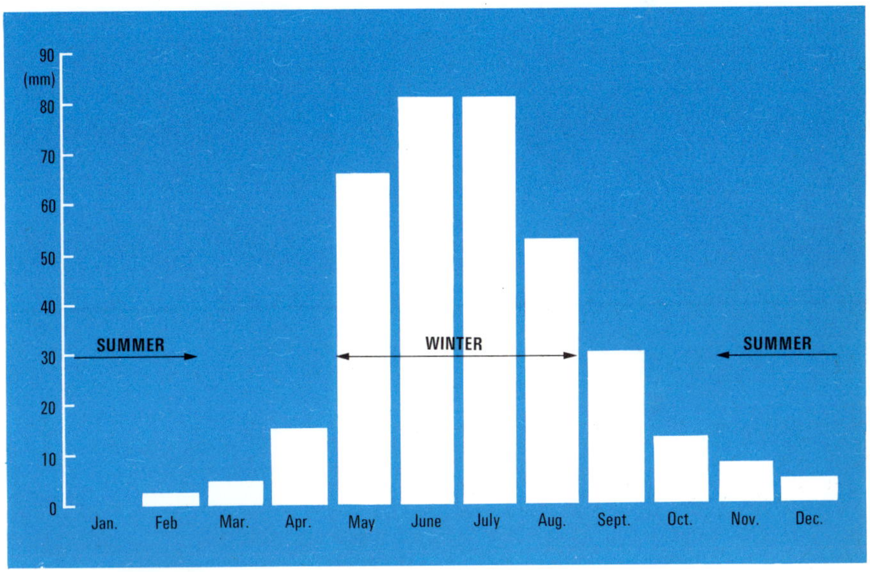

Fig. 63 Rainfall and seasons in Central Chile. The summer months are dry, most rain falls in winter. Compare this chart with others elsewhere in this book.

Corrugated iron heats up very rapidly, but cools just as quickly, so the people inside tend to feel many temperature changes. The iron roof is cheap, much lighter than tiles (so requiring less timber in the roof), and quite waterproof, but the house with such a roof is very noisy in rain. Which type of roof would be best suited to the climate?

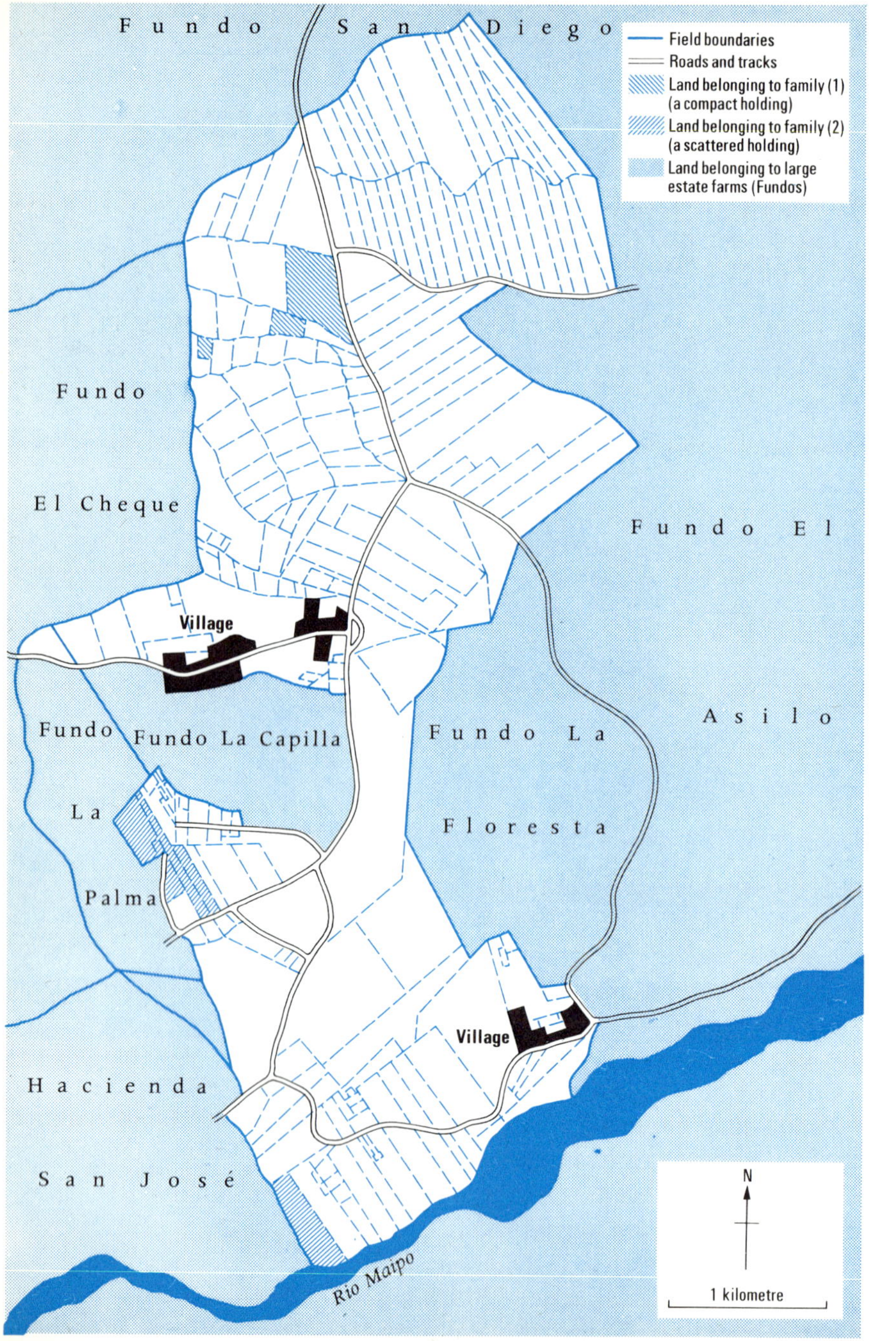

Fig. 64 Farms in the Cuncumen district of Central Chile. The farmers live in the villages, but their land is in small strips which may be in different areas. What advantages and disadvantages are there in having a scattered farm?

The house and the land it stands on belongs to the family. They pay no rent, and carry out all repairs to the property themselves. In addition, they own some farming land. The map (Fig. 64) shows how this land tends to be scattered about in different places. The district has various different types of soil; the idea of having the farm broken up in this way into small strips is so that each family has a roughly equal share of the good and bad land.

In this area of Chile many families still live in this way, their houses grouped in small villages with their small strips of farming land within walking distance.

Because the family own their own land they are called 'owner-cultivators'. They grow most of the food they need and keep animals for meat and milk, with chickens for eggs. When they travel to the city they may use the public bus, or a motor cycle.

Suggest ways in which an 'owner-cultivator' family might obtain cash for trips to town to buy things they cannot grow or make for themselves. Consider what they could do with any eggs, meat or crops, etc., they did not use themselves.

Around the villages, as the map shows, there are very large areas of land with

Photos. 77 and 78 A scene in Temuco Province, about 600 kilometres south of Santiago. The farmer is using oxen to draw his plough. The plough is of a new type, made in Japan, and replaces the very crude wooden plough that was used before. Note the thatched buildings in the background. In the second photograph the farmer and his younger brother are weeding cabbages which they will eventually take to market in the town of Temuco, for sale. In doing this they are following advice from the government experts. Previously they lived by 'subsistence' farming, growing food only for themselves, using most primitive methods and often finding it hard to make ends meet. Now, with cash from sales, they can afford better clothing and housing, more varied food, and can buy better farm tools.

names like 'Fundo San Diego', 'Fundo la Floresta' and 'Hacienda San José'. Even the smallest shown here, Fundo la Palma, is over two kilometres long, and most are far larger, too big for the map to include them. These are very large farms or ranches.

Such huge estates are very common all over South America, carrying different names in different countries; Estancias in Argentina, Fazendas in Brazil. Usually these big estates are owned by very wealthy families, some of whom have lived in the same place for many generations. In other cases the estate may belong to a company based in a city office with a manager to run the farm.

In Chile, however, things are rapidly changing. Some of the Fundos have been taken over by the government to be reorganized as collective farms. On a collective farm the land and buildings belong to the government and the farm workers hold meetings to discuss important matters and take decisions. The intention is that the farm shall be run for the benefit of the whole country, not just for one family or one company. Any profits made by the sale of crops are either used on the farm to improve living conditions for the workers or to buy modern machinery and equipment. Anything left over may go to the government to pay taxes. With this money the government can provide roads, new schools and hospitals—things which Chile has needed desperately for years.

To turn a big estate into a collective farm, however, is not enough by itself to ensure efficient farming. The land has to be well managed. The government of Chile is doing all it can, in conjunction with international bodies such as the Food and Agriculture Organisation of the United Nations, to bring farming methods up to date. The photographs show how this is done.

Photos. 79 and 80 The girls in these picture are at school. As well as normal classroom subjects they are learning to farm. Their school is at Macul, close to Santiago. When they leave school they will, as a rule, return to their family farms and will be able to introduce new methods. At another agricultural school near Temuco the girls learn, among other things, pig breeding and management.

Photo. 81 Young men from farms all over Chile come to the Santa Elena Training Centre to learn about modern farming methods. Here they are learning how to give an injection to a sick pig. When their studies are finished they will return to their home collective or other farm and in many cases will become farm managers and supervisors.

Photo. 82 Not many farms in Chile, in the old days, had machinery. Now it is becoming more common, and men have to learn how to use it and how to look after it and make repairs. A number of special training centres have been set up. Here the students are repairing a disc harrow which is used to cut up heavy soils to allow air to circulate and water to drain away. Leaning against the wall on the right is a spike harrow, which is like a large, heavy rake to break up the soil after ploughing. Close to the camera also against this wall is a heavy plough. In the background are tractors.

Photo. 83 Science is called in to assist Chilean farmers to improve their methods. The grass in this area used to be poor and sparse, but a new type of plant, 'Atriplex', has been introduced and is growing well. In the foreground experts examine the growth while in the distance sheep graze in pastures which did not exist before.

Photo. 84 Soil erosion. In times of heavy rain the small stream on the left in this picture becomes a raging torrent. It has carved out for itself a deep gulley, carrying away soil and rock. If nothing is done to check it the gulley will grow deeper and wider as time goes on until most of the soil will have been stripped off the land. From a gulley such as this other gullies may grow until a whole area is cut up and eroded into desert-like rocky hills. The Chilean government is making great efforts to prevent further erosion. The local people have been paid to dig ditches across the slope, so that water running downhill will be checked and slowed down, giving it time to soak into the soil instead of flowing across it. Atriplex grasses have been planted so that the plant roots will bind the soil together and help to hold it in place. In time, if these measures succeed, sheep will be able to graze on land that otherwise would become quite useless.

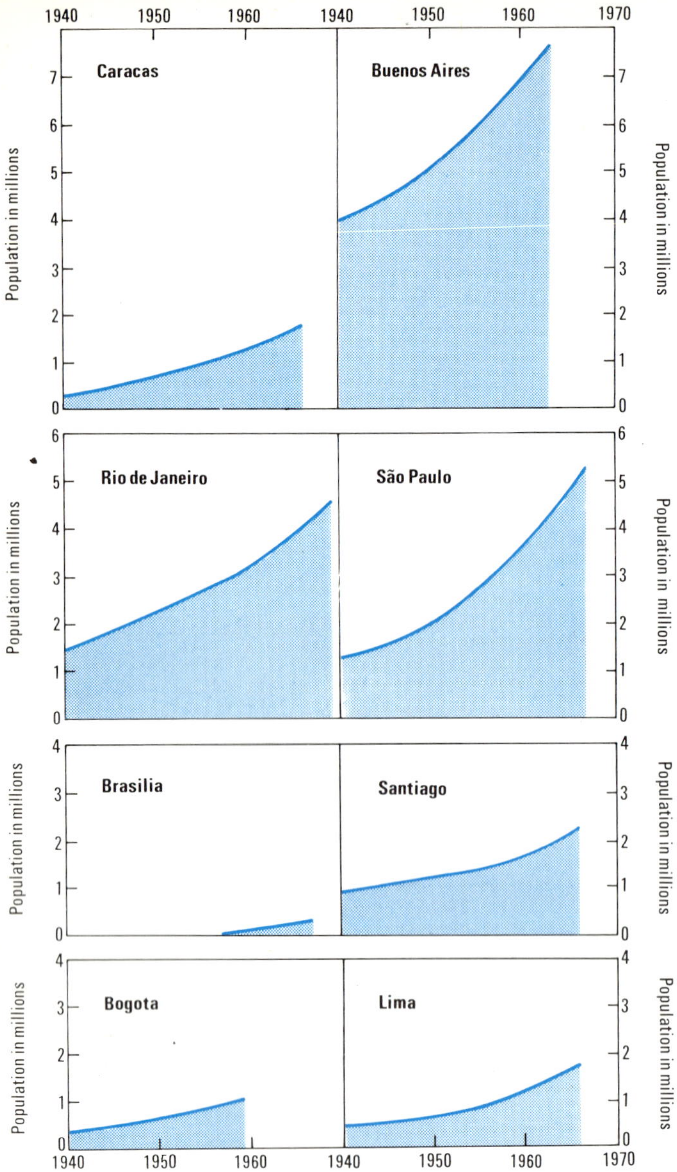

Fig. 65 The growth of population in eight leading cities of South America. The steeper the slope of the graph, the faster the growth of the city. Use a reference library to fill in the most recent years.

8 Growing Cities of South America

The nearest large city to the farmers described in the last chapter is Santiago. Look at the graphs in Fig. 65. What have these cities in common with Santiago?

All the cities marked on the map (Fig. 66) are growing, some very rapidly indeed. Which is the largest city of those marked? Which is the fastest growing?

São Paulo

São Paulo is increasing by a quarter of a million people each year; if this continues by 2000 A.D. it will have nearly 14 million, and will be bigger than any city in the world at the present time. The graph (Fig. 67) indicates that São Paulo began as a small town over a hundred years ago. It grew fairly steadily at first, passing the million mark in the late nineteen-thirties. Since then it has gone ahead very rapidly indeed—doubling between 1936 and 1950, doubling again between 1950 and 1960, and the way things are going it seems likely to double again between 1960 and 1970. Brazilians in some ways are very proud of São Paulo—but in other ways they are rather frightened by it. How much more will this huge city grow? Should it be allowed to go on getting bigger and bigger? What will happen if it goes on

Fig. 66 Some leading cities of South America

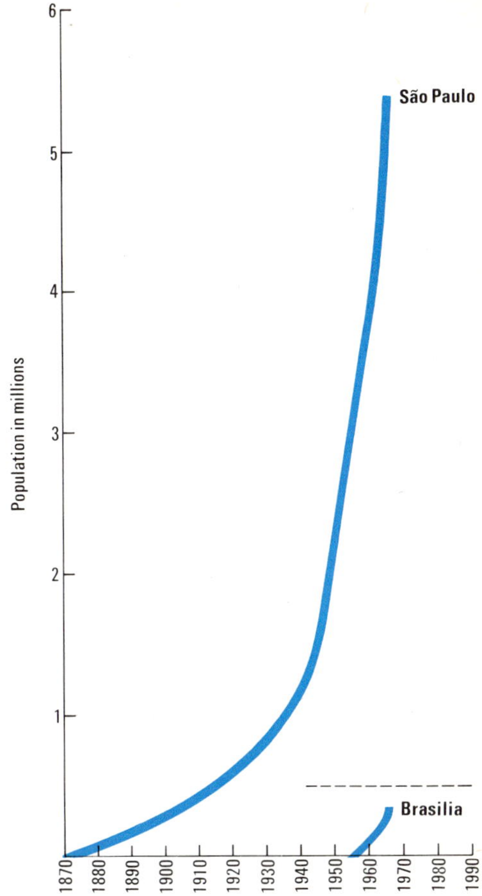

Fig. 67 Graph showing the growth of population of Brasilia and São Paulo. The broken line indicates the planner's intended limit for Brasilia. However, the growth of new shanty towns has upset the plan.

doubling every ten years? Surely it has to stop growing sometime?

In São Paulo a new building is completed somewhere in the city every day. Half the industries of Brazil are in this city, and a third of all the electric power produced in the country is used in São Paulo. The nearby port of Santos which serves Sao Paulo handles a quarter of all Brazilian shipping trade. But the growth is too rapid even though huge amounts of money are spent on improvements. Often houses are knocked down to make room in the city centre for office blocks, but already there are not enough houses. David Crease wrote:

São Paulo is much admired but little loved. It combines the disadvantages common to most large cities—noise, rush, stink, danger—with some specific to Brazil. Public services lag far behind the boom in industrial and commercial development. The telephone service if you can find a telephone, is uncertain. In sudden rainstorms sewers block and children drown in their beds. The motor car factories choke the broken streets with their products. São Paulo cannot stop, say the Paulistanos (citizens of São Paulo). They might add,

Photo. 85 Traffic jam in a main street in São Paulo

Photo 86 The central district of São Paulo. Office blocks and skyscrapers. But where do the people live?

cannot stop to think. Health, education, street lighting, and paving—the city rushes ahead without them.

The photographs show two contrasting sides of South American cities—in the centre—tall skyscrapers, office blocks, traffic jams—but on the outskirts, huge slum towns:

Dismal and tumbledown wooden shacks. Home here for a family is one room, perhaps with partitions to screen space for cooking and sleeping. There are no street lights, piped water, drains, bus stops or other such works.

Wealth and poverty run side by side. In São Paulo there is hope for some slum-dwellers—the government is spending large amounts on new housing estates but the rents charged for the new houses are too high for many wage-earners. And the city grows too fast at present for planners and builders to keep up.

Photo. 87 Backyard in a poor district of Rio de Janeiro

Photo. 88 These slums are in Valparaiso, Chile.

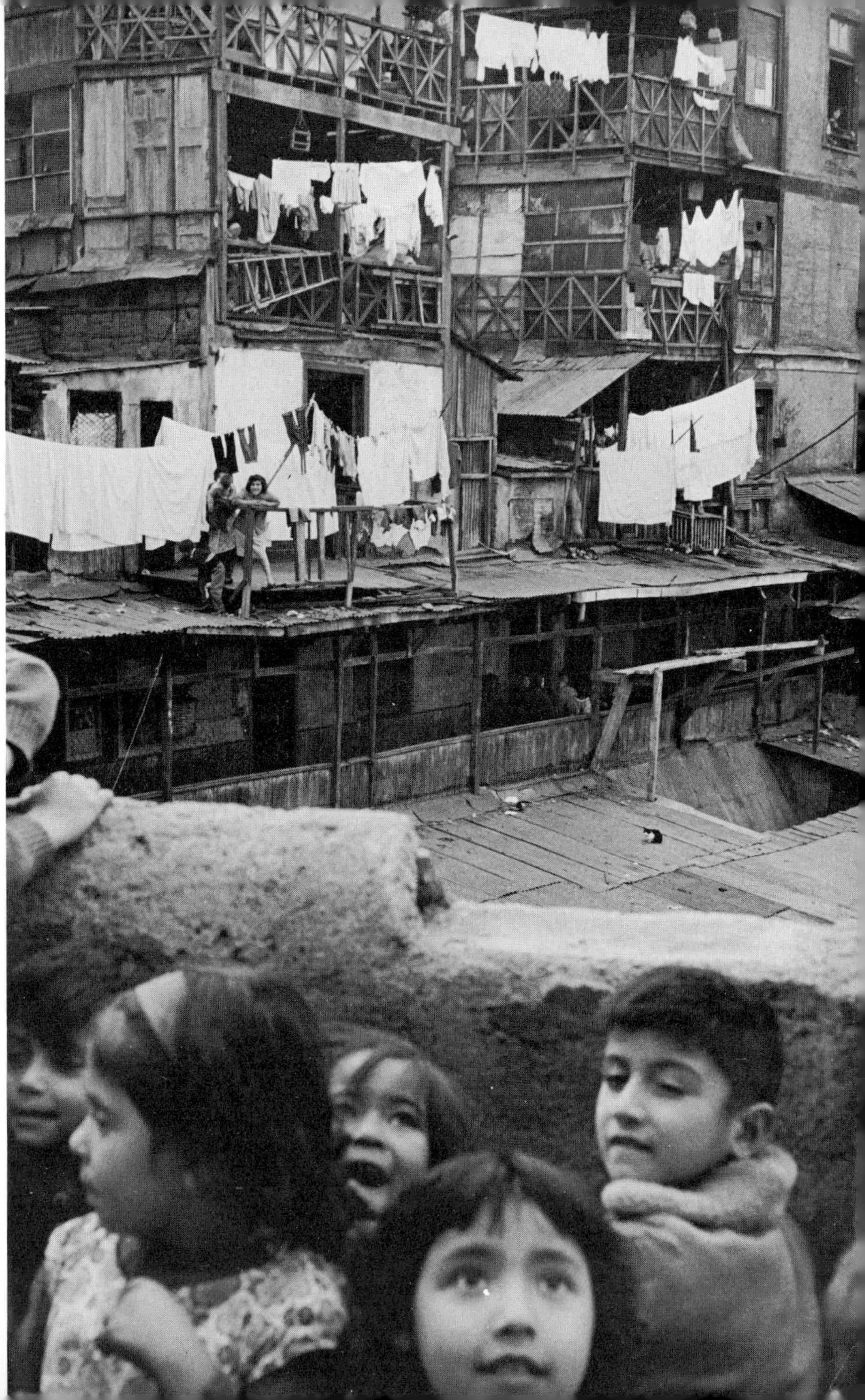

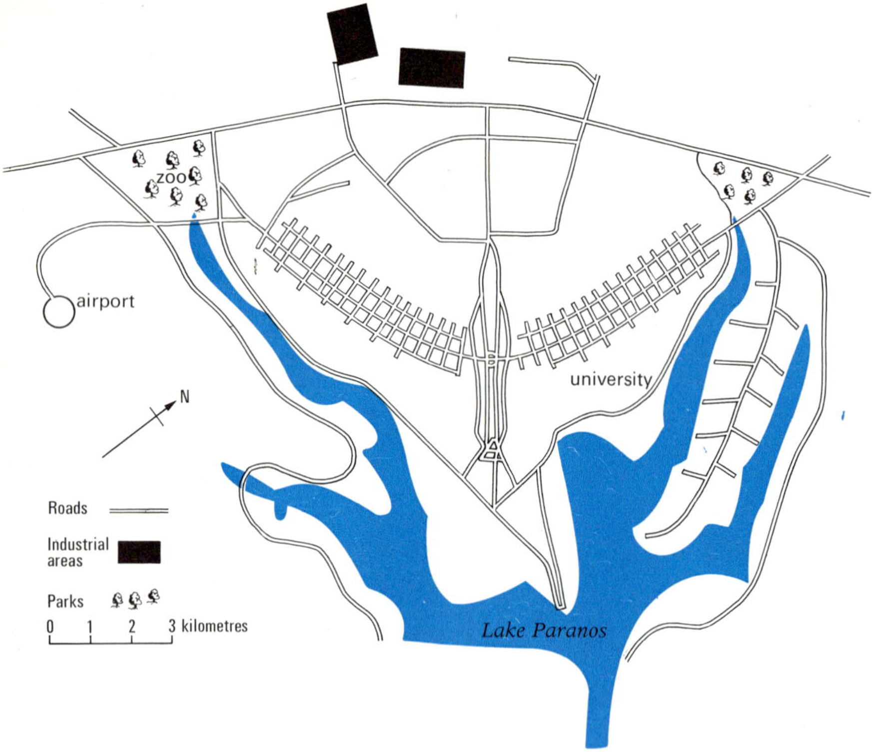

Fig. 68 Street plan of Brasilia, a city built to a definite plan

Brasilia

In its way, Brasilia, although much smaller, is even more remarkable than São Paulo. Notice that the graph for Brasilia (Fig. 67) started only in 1956. Before that year, there was nothing at Brasilia at all—it did not even have a name. There was simply a huge area of empty country, much of it without even farms or 'fazendas' in the interior of Brazil. Then in came hundreds of surveyors, engineers, and builders who set up their wooden huts and got to work. The bulldozers scooped out pits for the foundations, concrete mixers churned, and within months the big buildings began to appear.

Four years after the start, the President of Brazil moved from the old capital, Rio de Janeiro, to his new palace in Brasilia. The government offices moved too, and in April 1960 a grand ceremony was held. Brasilia was declared the new capital city of Brazil. Look at the photographs on pages 100–103, which show Brasilia today, and then remember that only a few years ago there was no building in this area.

To anyone visiting the region after a period away it would look as if a whole city had been transported by magic and planted in the open country. In truth, Brasilia has been planted, almost in the same way as a gardener might deliberately plant a tree. Compare the two maps (Fig. 68 and 69). What sort of pattern do the main roads of São Paulo make? The roads tend to run outwards in several directions from the centre, but often they swing about from side to side, and sometimes they seem to double back or run off in some strange direction. This sort of pattern of roads is very common in cities which have grown over a long period from small beginnings. At the start, some of the roads were little tracks through the fields, used only by

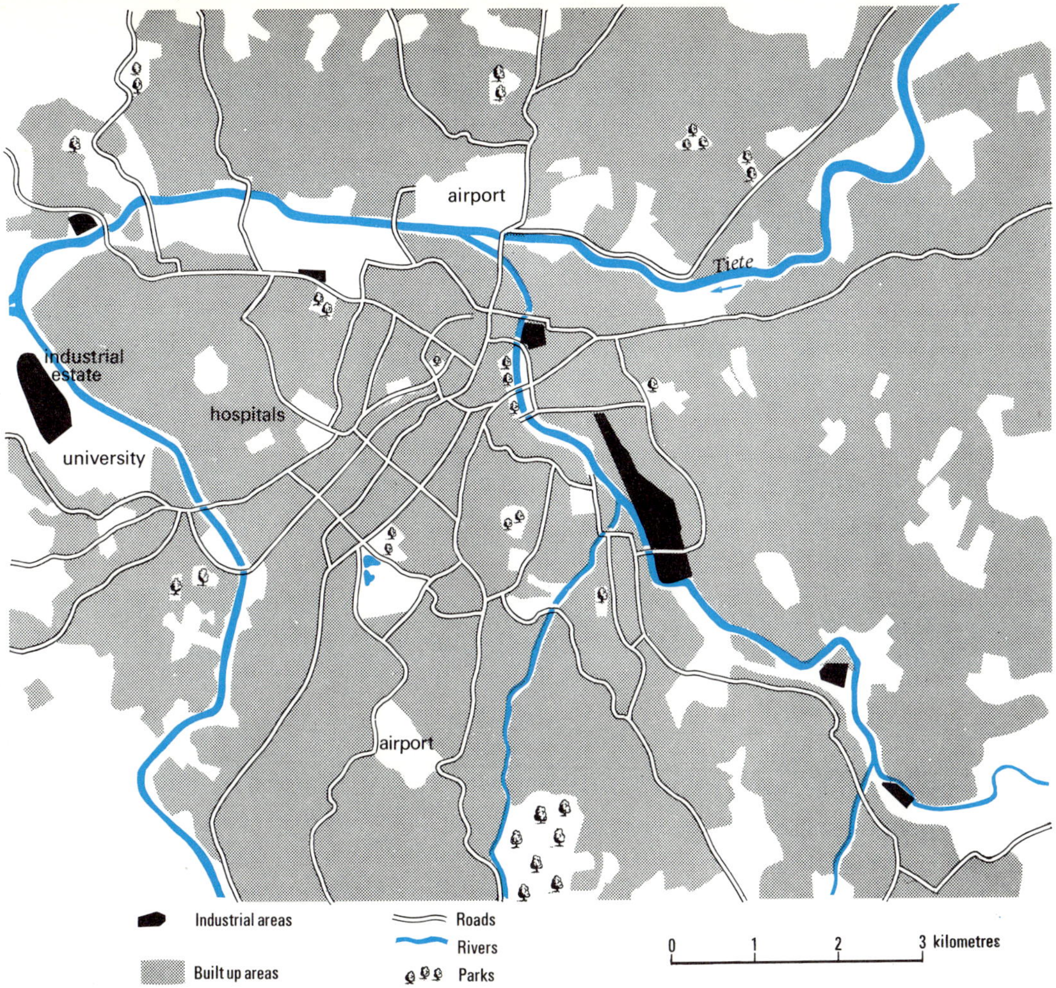

Fig. 69 Street plan of São Paulo, a city that has grown without a plan

farmers on their way to market with wheeled carts carrying coffee beans, or driving herds of cattle to the railway. As time went on such tracks became busier until it became necessary to lay a hard surface of gravel and fill in any pot-holes made by heavy rains of the wet season. Then as the city expanded the roads had to be properly re-laid and tarred, and now some of the old tracks carry thousands of motor vehicles every hour. But they still follow the ancient lines which were trodden out by the country folk a hundred years ago.

But obviously the pattern of roads and buildings in Brasilia were drawn out on paper first, and then built to this definite plan. Anyone looking at Brasilia can see this. Some people think this city was de-

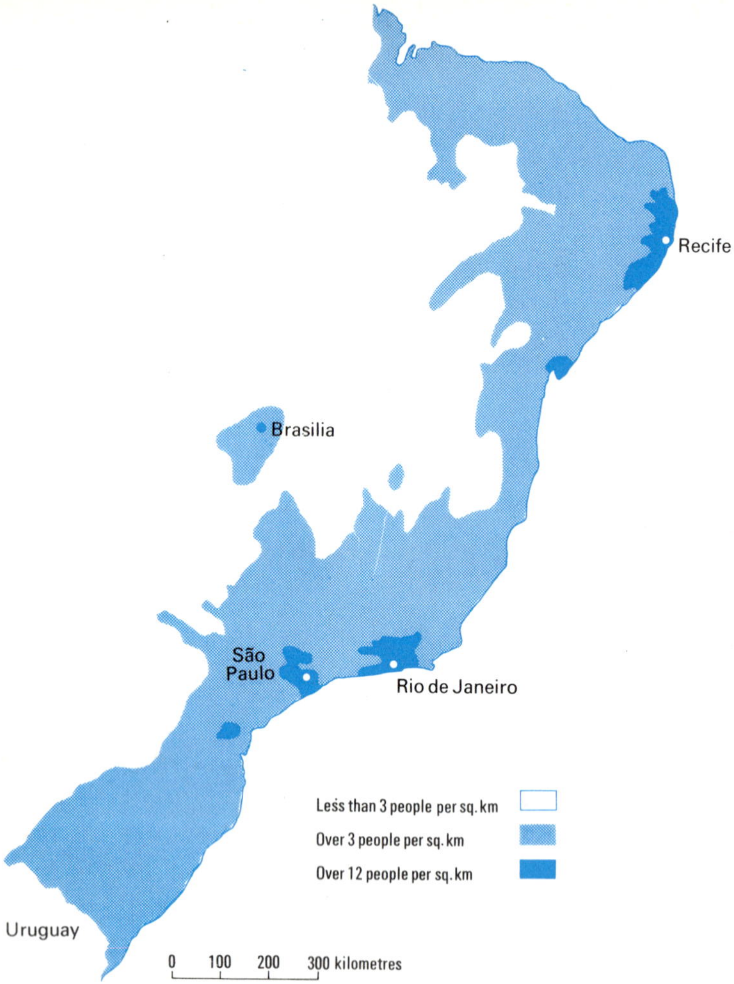

Fig. 70 Population of Brazil

signed to look like a modern aeroplane with swept wings, others see a bow and arrow. The man who actually drew this plan was called Lucio Costa, and it seems he did not really intend it to be either a bow or an aeroplane—he saw it as a kind of cross with curved arms. Afterwards he wrote: 'Basically it arose from the elementary gesture of one who marks or takes possession of a place; the sign of the cross itself.' Costa drew his curved cross on the map and now there stands the capital city of Brazil.

Of course Lucio Costa alone could not decide to build a new city by himself. What happened was this. When Brazil became an independent country, breaking away from Portuguese rule, in 1822, the leaders of the new government thought the country should have a new capital city which would show that they were no longer ruled by Europeans. The Portuguese had ruled from Rio de Janeiro, and for a very long time this ancient and beautiful city remained as the centre of government. But always at the back of the people's mind was the idea of a new capital.

Nothing was actually done about it until President Juscelino Kubitschek da Oliviera in 1956 decided that the time had come. One reason for his decision was his hope to be remembered for ever as the man who put the old idea into practice, but there were other important reasons as well. Study the population map of Brazil (Fig. 70). It is a huge country; the fifth largest in area in the world. But enormous areas are almost empty of people, the population is mainly in the south-east—as we have already seen, some seven millions in São Paulo alone, and millions more in Rio de Janeiro. The Kubitschek government thought it necessary to encourage people to move inland to occupy the empty country of Minais Gerais. One way they might have done this would have been to offer cheap land to farmers—there is good country for cattle, or sheep, and many crops can be grown. But if farmers were to make a living they would need to sell their produce and this would mean that new roads and railways would be needed to get the goods to the cities. A scheme for new roads was drafted but this was not enough. The idea of an entirely new city was very attractive, and President Kubitschek announced a competition for the best design. His friend, architect Oscar Niemayer, helped in the judging of the plans, and Lucio Costa won. There was a great deal of fierce argument about the whole idea, especially when people realized how much the project was going to cost Brazil. But Kubitschek talked, argued and persuaded and the city went ahead. Many people think the whole scheme was wrong. Whatever they think, Brasilia is there and is growing. When Costa drew his first plan, he was instructed to provide a city of just half a million people. There is a broken line on the graph on page 93 to show this limit. In theory the city should grow to that size and then grow no further. But homes were not planned and built for the labourers who built the central city. Although the city itself is still closely following Costa's plan, a number of 'satellite' towns have grown up in the open country outside the planned area, Fig. 71.

Even if the capital itself is held down to half a million, it is almost certain that these other towns will expand until, perhaps, they all run together to form another huge metropolis like São Paulo. Kubitschek's idea to populate the interior will then have succeeded, but in a different way from his expectations.

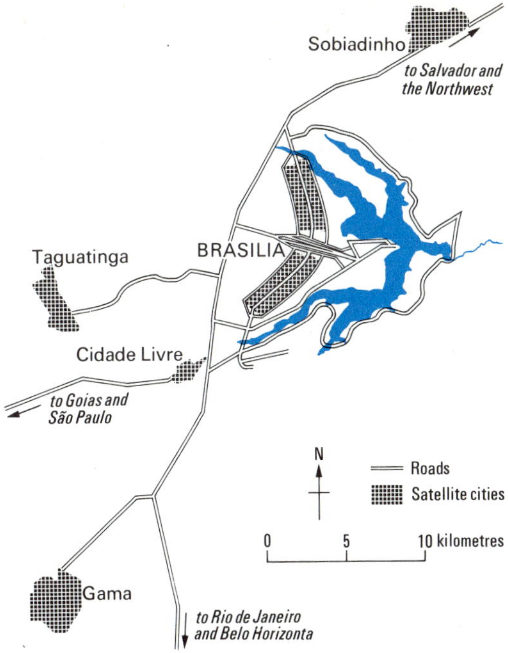

Fig. 71 Brasilia, with the unplanned shanty towns which have grown up. Where will the people of such towns find work? How far from Brasilia itself are they?

Photo. 89 The centre of Brasilia. The city stands on flat land with no limit to its growth.

Photo. 90 Bus station designed for Brasilia by the architect, Lucio Costa

Photo. 91 A modern office block in Brasilia. Do you suppose the people who work here are well paid? What evidence is there in the photograph to help you decide?

Photo. 92 Market is held on Saturday and Sunday mornings in the centre of Brasilia. Workers who come mainly from the north-east part of the country can buy provisions they are used to buying back home.

Photo. 93 A photograph of Brasilia today. In the central area there are pleasant lawns and pedestrian footpaths. The size of the young trees gives some idea of how long the city has existed.

Photos. 94 and 95 The photographs opposite were taken in the shanty towns which have grown up near to Brasilia but which were not part of the planned city. What sort of jobs do you think the people living here might have? Read pages 98–99 to find some clues. If you had been planning a city like Brasilia, can you think of any ways in which you could have planned for the shanty town dwellers?

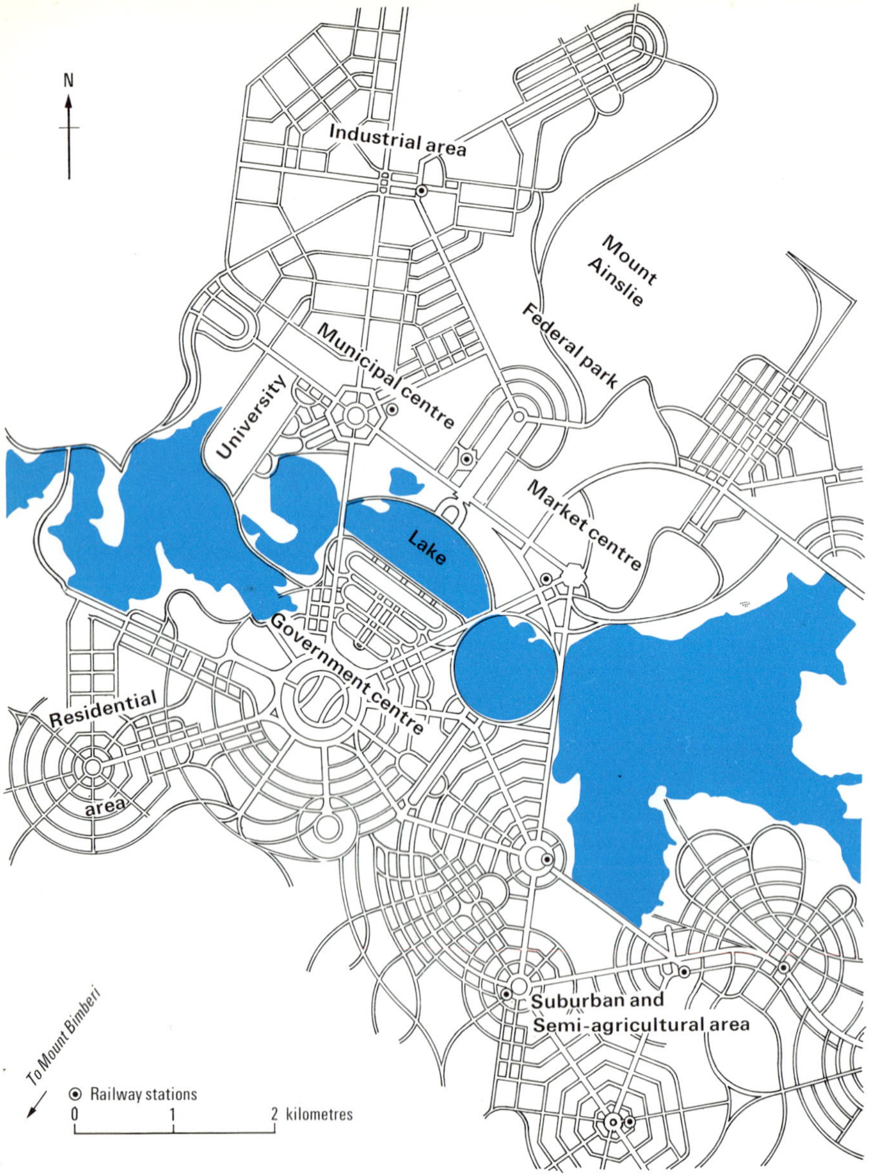

Fig. 72 Canberra—capital of Australia. A planned city, built in a highland region which was previously almost uninhabited.

Notes on Planned Cities

São Paulo is a city which, like most others in the world, for instance, Kanpur, Calcutta, Singapore, Accra, has grown up without any set plan. As it grows, problems arise which were not foreseen, and the people have to cope with them as best they can. Sometimes they can keep up with change, but often change is too rapid.

Discuss the idea of planning a city right from the beginning.

What sorts of things would you have to consider? Where would the people come from? What work would they do?

Would it be best to start building houses first, or should there be roads to begin with?

Would it be any good putting up factories before there was anywhere for people to live?

Do you know of any 'new towns' where this idea of the 'planned city' has been tried?

Study the group of city plans given here. Find each one in your atlas.

Compare these deliberately planned cities with other city plans in this book and with any other city plans you can find. Nearly all cities have had some planning at some stage, but often the planners could not see far enough into the future to make allowances for everything that might happen.

For instance, cities drawn out hundreds of years ago were not intended for motor cars, and even fifty years ago very few people imagined that airports would be necessary. Nowadays planners like Costa in Brazil know that cars and airports are essential, but who can say what a modern city will need in another hundred years? You might find it interesting to sketch out a few plans of your own for cities of the future.

Will people still have motor cars?

Is it possible they might use small aeroplanes or helicopters instead? Possibly hover-craft will be much more common or maybe there will be moving footpaths.

Will everyone live in flats, or will there still be room for houses with gardens?

You will have to allow space for recreation—if your city is to have a million people, how many sports grounds, football stadia, etc., will the city need? How many theatres, cinemas? Perhaps there won't be any such things in a hundred years? That doesn't seem very likely, but no-one foresaw television when plans for cities were drawn up in ancient times.

Look at some of the 'ideal' cities that planners imagined in the past, and think how well, or how badly, they worked out.

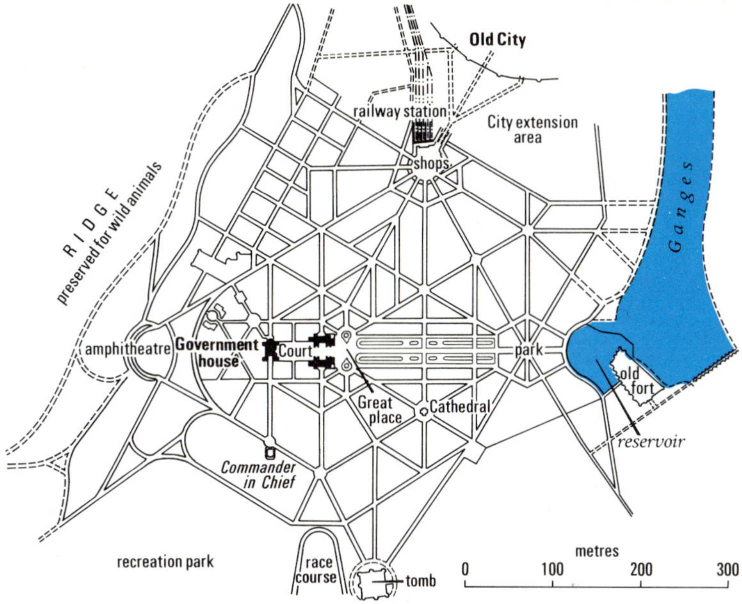

Fig. 73 New Delhi—the capital of India. A planned city built in the 20th century

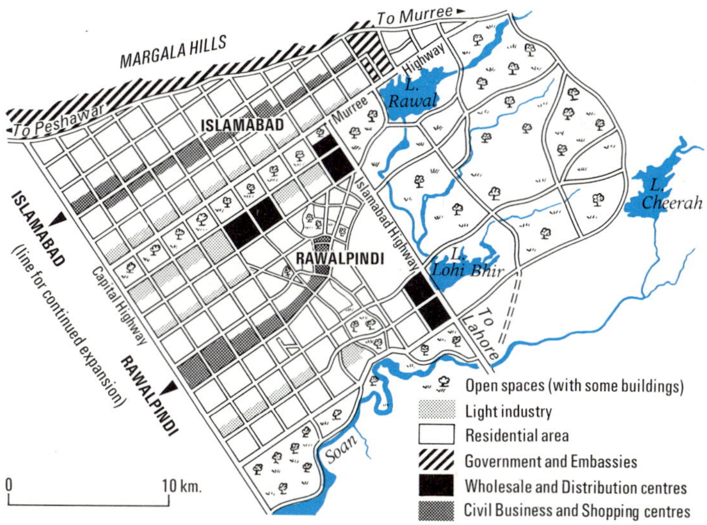

Fig. 74 Plan of Islamabad—capital of Pakistan

Photo. 96 Adelaide seen from the hills east of the city. Note in the distance the tall city buildings, and in the foreground the typical bungalow housing.

Photo. 97 An aerial view of Adelaide. Note the hills in the background and the parklands close to the city centre. Since this photograph was taken several more office blocks have been built.

9 City with a Plan

In the previous chapter several city plans were shown. But the city plan is only one aspect of city building. You should ask yourself, why have cities at all? Why can't everyone live apart from everyone else, in the open country or in small villages? This is a question which you will find very difficult to answer. You might start off by making a list of all the jobs you can think of which have to be done by getting large numbers of people together.

Some of the very first motor cars were built in small 'backyard' workshops by one or two men. They had to do every job themselves—they had to know how to make the engine, the chassis, the body, tyres, gears, etc. Later on, when motor cars became very popular and important, the little workshops became too small, and more people had to be brought in to help in what soon became a factory. In a factory a workman does not usually need to know how to do every job. One man is an engine designer, for example, another makes parts for the engine, another assembles the parts, and another fits the whole engine into the car, while others work in the same way on gears, wheels, body, and so on. This kind of 'mass production' is very important in our times,

Photos. 98 and 99 The statue of Colonel William Light situated on a hill in North Adelaide, and the inscription on the base of Light's statue

and factories of all kinds are needed. A car factory needs steel, other metals, electrical apparatus, tyres, plastics, and many other things that go into cars. So other factories to make all these things are often found near car factories. And the workers need to live near the factories, so they must have houses. So there is work for builders, plumbers, and electricians. Then the wives need shops to buy food and goods for the family, and the children need schools; there will have to be doctors, dentists, hospitals, and usually various kinds of government offices and so the list gets longer and longer.

As a rule, nobody worked it all out in advance; the small motor car workshop might have been started by some young man in his spare time just because he was very keen on motor cars. Something like this did happen in the ancient city of Oxford. A young man called Morris, working in a cycle shop, began building motor cars in his spare time. His cars worked well. Today Oxford is a large city and the motor car factory is one of the largest in Britain. Even so Oxford does not compare in size with another motor-car city, Detroit, in the U.S.A. Detroit too, owes its existence almost to one man—another famous inventor, Henry Ford. But Detroit and Oxford were towns already before motor cars were thought of.

The city we shall be studying in this chapter began very differently from Oxford and Detroit, although it is, as you will see, getting more like them as time goes on. In some ways it began like Brasilia, but over a hundred years earlier.

Exploration

The photographs above show the statue of Colonel William Light, as it stands today, looking out over the city of Adelaide in South Australia. The inscription on the statue's base is worth reading, for it tells how one man planted a city. In the years 1829–1830 exploration of Australia was still in an early stage. The coasts were fairly well known but the interior was empty. A great explorer, Captain Charles Sturt, made a long journey by boat down the Murray River, and reported that there was good land for settlement in South Australia. It was decided in London to set up a new colony. A navy Captain, John Hindmarsh, was appointed governor of the new colony and an army Colonel, William Light, was sent to the area to make maps

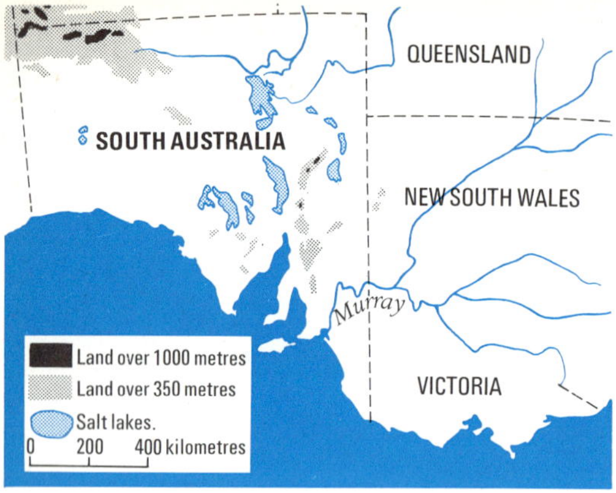

Fig. 75 South Australia—this map shows high ground. The salt lakes are a sign of a very hot and dry climate in those areas. The new city needed a harbour, to protect ships from southerly storms.

Fig. 77 The position of South Australia in the Australian continent. In Colonel Light's time Sydney was already important but Melbourne was a very small village. There were a few other settled places in what later became Tasmania, Western Australia and Queensland.

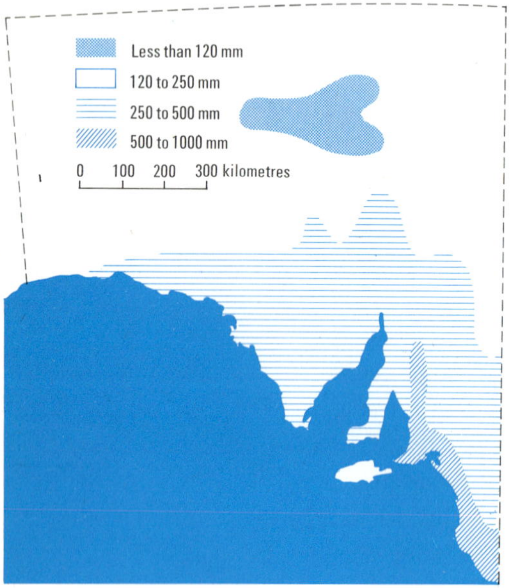

Fig. 76 A rainfall map of South Australia. This is the driest state in a dry continent. A city always needs great quantities of water.

Fig. 78 South Australia showing some possible sites for the city. Some were exposed to storms from the south. Some were too hard to reach from the eastern side. Some were in dry or semi-desert country. The River Murray was not suitable for ships because sand and silt blocked the mouth. Did Light choose well?

and to decide where the capital city should be. Except for a few whaling boats which sometimes stayed for a few weeks on the coasts, no-one had any idea what the country would be like—but Colonel Light did know, before he had finished his plan, what the new town would be called. It was named Adelaide after the English queen, and its main street after King William.

Photo. 100 North Terrace, Adelaide

Photo. 101 King William Street, Adelaide's main street. Find this street and North Terrace on Light's original plan for the city.

Choosing a site for a new city

Look carefully at the maps of South Australia given here (Figs. 75 to 78). Suppose you were Colonel Light and had to choose a place for a completely new city. Where would you choose? You should find this decision much easier than Light did, for he had no maps like these. All he knew was the rough outline of the coast and such reports as sailors had written, from time to time, in their ships' log books, about where there was fresh water, or a good harbour. These were some of the things that Light had to think of:

1 There must be fairly flat land for building.
2 The city must have plenty of fresh water.
3 There should be a good harbour.
4 There must be good farming land near.
5 There should be good routes to the other parts of Australia, particularly to Sydney, already important by Light's time.
6 There should be plenty of room for the city to grow bigger.

Without looking ahead in the book, where do you think Colonel Light put his city?

On the map (Fig. 78) several possible places have been marked. Light went to look at most of these. Which one do you think was best? Now look at the map on page 112 (Fig. 80) and see if you agreed with him. There is nothing anyone can do now, if you think Light was wrong. Adelaide today is exactly where he put it! There are smaller towns at all the other marked places—perhaps if you had been Colonel Light, one of those other places would be called Adelaide today. Would your choice have been as good a place for the city?

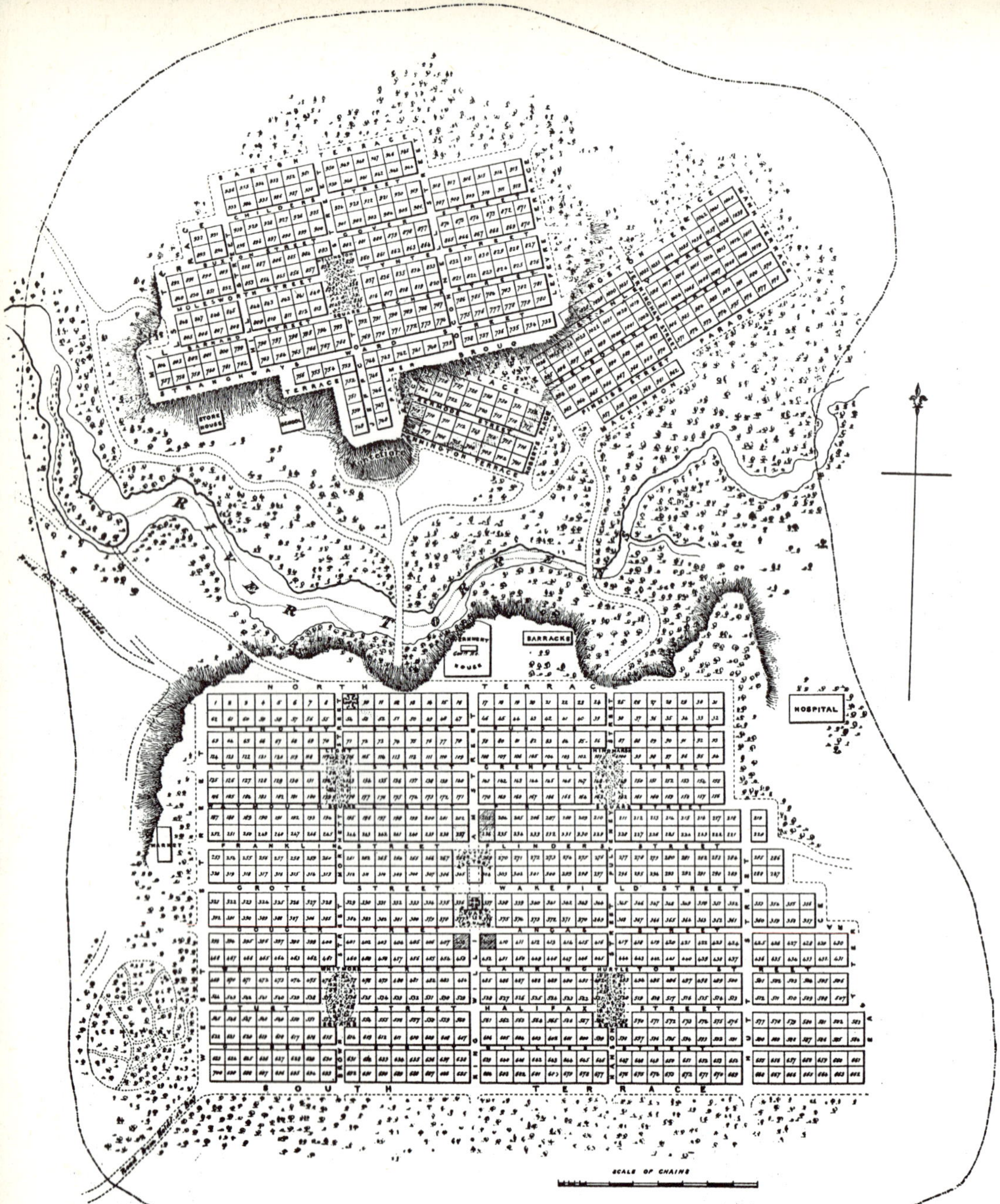

Fig. 79 On the left is Colonel Light's original plan for the centre of Adelaide. On the right is an aerial photograph taken recently. The street plan and main outline of the city is exactly as Light imagined it, but there are many details he could not have expected. Pick out on the photograph some of the more obvious and important differences and try to explain them. For example, why did Light fail to plan for a railway station? Can you see the station and goods yards on the photograph?

Photo. 102 City of Adelaide viewed from the air. Compare this photograph with Colonel Light's original plan for the city centre.

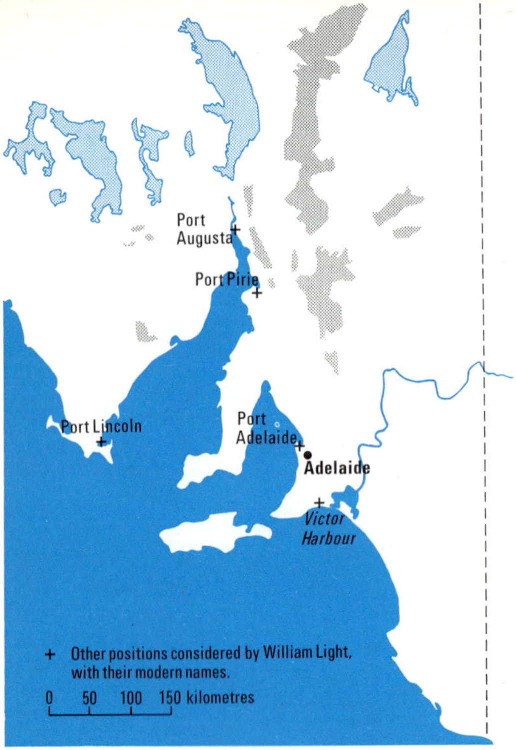

Fig. 80 The position of Adelaide in South Australia, with other places which were seriously considered for the site. Light thought that Victor Harbour was too exposed to storms, Port Lincoln too cut off from the landward side, Port Augusta and Port Pirie in too dry a region. Sand and gravel banks prevented ships sailing up the Murray, so the river had little importance at that time.

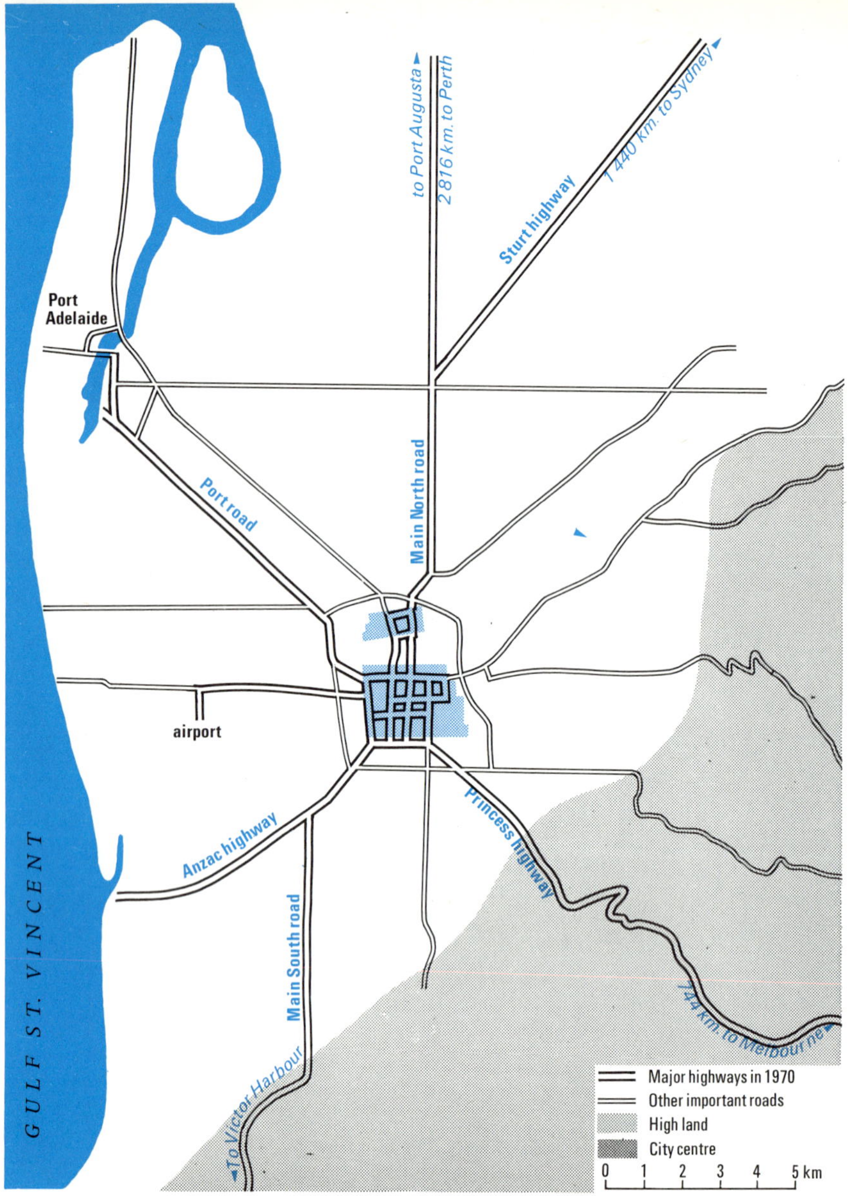

Fig. 81 Main roads leading from Adelaide in 1971

Fig. 82 The growth of Adelaide. Each map shows the area covered by buildings in the year mentioned. In 1880, except for the port and the central city, there was little built up area. Expansion from 1939 to 1970 has been very great.

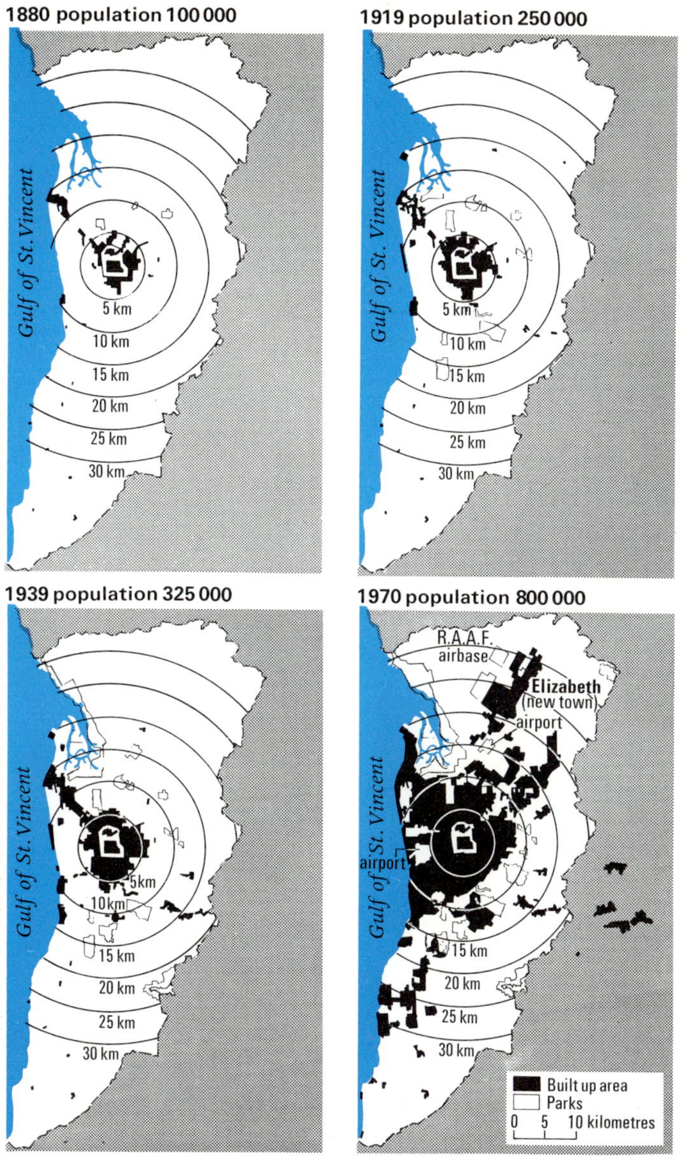

Planning a city

The map on the previous page shows how Light drew out his plans for the new city. Compare it with the plans shown on pages 104–105. Is it like any of them? When it came to planning the main roads, Light had to think of many things again. What sort of road plan from the city would you have planned? Remember that the easiest way for goods and travellers to move about in those days was by sea and on rivers. You would need a good road from the city to the port. Then you would want roads for movement inland to the River Murray—across the plains to the north and through the hills to the south-east. Try sketching a plan of your own, then compare it with what Light actually did (Fig. 79). If he was badly wrong it would be very difficult to change the city now. He laid out roads, drew maps, and the city has followed these lines.

Most people think Light's choice of site, and his street plan, very good. Nothing is ever perfect, but Adelaide is a very beautiful city; the ring of parks that Colonel Light laid out is still there and his fine, broad streets in the city centre are lined with tall buildings and shops. The next series of maps (Fig. 82) shows how the city grew.

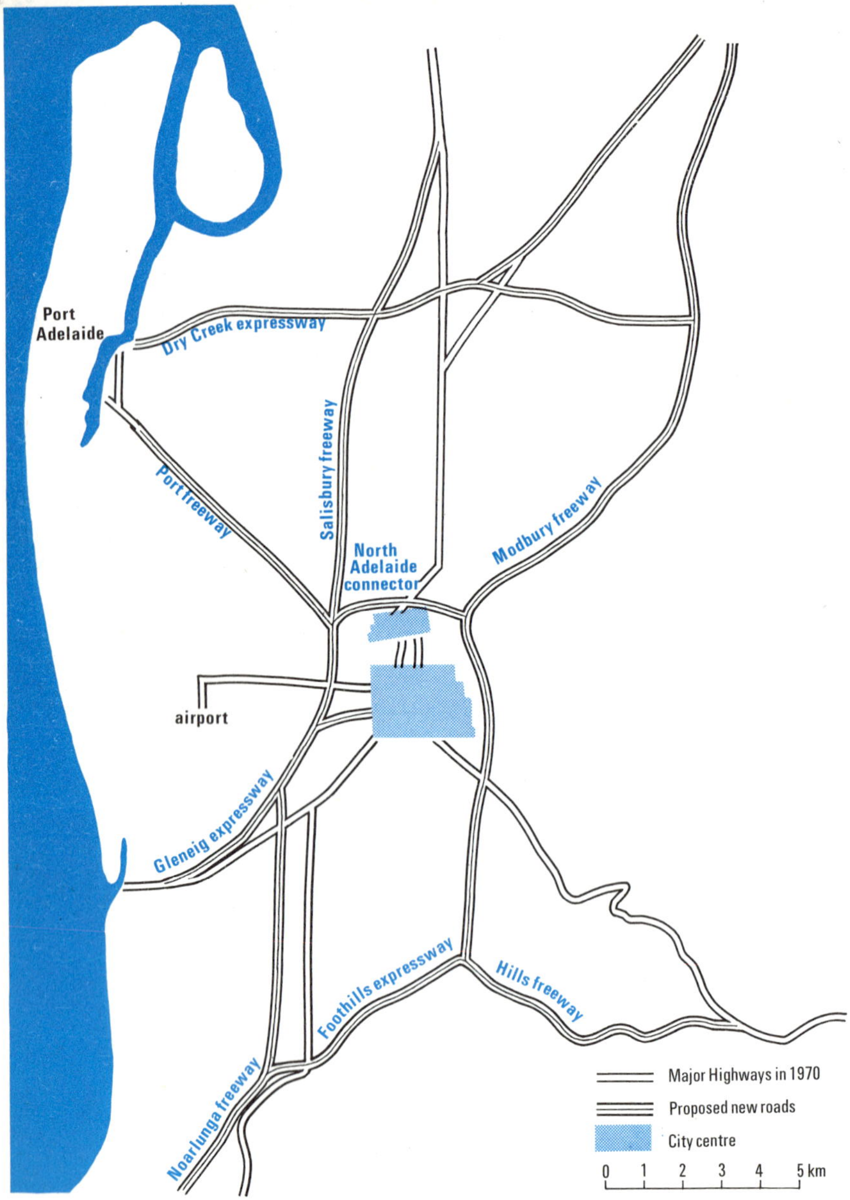

Fig. 83 Proposed motorways and express ways for Adelaide. It has been decided that some of these at least will be built in the next few years, but others will probably not be required.

Modern traffic

Colonel Light certainly did not know that one day aeroplanes would be important, and he would be very surprised to see that Adelaide now has two civil aerodromes on the flat land between the hills and the sea, and also a large military air base. But he would probably be even more astonished if he could see the motor traffic in his city. In his day horses and carts, bullock teams pulling great wagons, stagecoaches, and boats were the main means of transport. He even planned for a canal to the port, but this was never built. Instead, today, there are over 200 000 vehicles in Adelaide, and as the city gets still bigger, this will increase to well over 400 000. Soon the city will, like many others in the world, be suffering from traffic jams unless something can be done to prevent them.

The South Australian Government is faced now with the traffic problem. What should they do? There are various possibilities. They could, perhaps, find some way of stopping people using cars in the city. Perhaps they would have to erect barriers across the roads and allow through only buses. Then people would have to park their cars near the barriers, on the way to

Photo. 103 Making television tubes

the city, and take the bus.

Can you see any difficulties that would arise with this scheme? Some are listed below:

1 There would have to be plenty of parking space near the barriers.
2 Many more buses would have to be built and drivers found for them.
3 Shops and businesses in the city would not be able to get deliveries of goods, etc., by road.
4 Customers might not bother to go into the city shops, new shops would probably be built in the suburbs, while the city centre might gradually die.

You may be able to think of other difficulties yourself. Another possible way of solving the problem might be simply to make all the city roads wider, turning them into one way streets, etc. Some of the difficulties here would be:

1 A lot of important buildings would have to be knocked down—this would cost a great deal because new buildings would have to be erected.
2 More parking space would be needed.

You may be able to suggest others ways of overcoming the problems of this city. Any answer is hard, but whatever is decided by the planners will have a big effect on the future. Do you think the map (Fig. 83) shown here is the best answer? It shows a whole series of entirely new roads—motorways or freeways and expressways which the South Australian government hopes to build during the next few years. To build them as shown, many houses and other buildings will have to be demolished. Houses which at present stand in their own quiet gardens may have a great freeway running within a few yards; some of the open spaces in the suburbs will have to go, and in the city itself there will have to be more parking spaces. Is this scheme the best? Can you work out a better one?

The proposals for freeways in Adelaide have been very strongly attacked by many people who fear that the new highways, while cutting their way through and ruining some pleasant suburbs, will still fail to help the traffic situation. When there is a freeway, people tend to use their cars more and possibly some families who did not have them before buy cars because the freeway seems to be a quicker way of getting about than the bus or train. So in this way the freeways make more traffic, and the jams become bigger than ever. Yet the city centre

Photo. 104 Aerial view of Elizabeth, looking south towards Adelaide

still has not enough parking space for all the cars that pour in, so soon buildings are knocked down to make way for car parks. Then, as time goes on and things get worse, no one can face the journey into town any more, and the shops in the centre get fewer and fewer customers and close down. The city centre gradually chokes to death.

Perhaps the best answer would be to build more houses and tall blocks of flats in the centre of the city, so that people living there did not have to travel so far to get to their work. You may already have noticed how few such tall blocks there are in Adelaide. Nearly everyone lives in detached bungalows in quite large gardens, whereas in London and in most European capitals, for example, the houses are much closer together and many people do live in flats.

The truth is, no one really knows what the best answer to these problems is. They are matters for serious discussion. Every large city in the world has similar troubles or worse ones—in India there are slums and overcrowding; in Los Angeles the freeways have already destroyed most of the city centre and there are so many motor car exhausts pouring fumes into the air that a poisonous fog forms over the whole city. Adelaide, too, is beginning to suffer from this pollution problem. Brasilia is a new city which has difficulty simply in getting started at all; São Paulo is growing too fast; Adelaide is smaller than any of these but is worried about the future.

For discussion: What are the problems of your city? Can you work out any plans to overcome them?

There are very few really poor people in Adelaide. Some of the houses are rather small, and were built from corrugated iron many years ago with no bathrooms or modern amenities, but as time goes on more and more of these are disappearing, pulled down to make room for modern office blocks and flats. Almost everywhere else any ordinary family can expect to have a house with at least four or five rooms and a

Photo. 105 The town centre of Elizabeth with Hotel Elizabeth and Post Office in the foreground

garden. When families do fall on hard times, there are various government schemes and private charities which exist to help them. Elderly folk have a pension, which is not very much but at least they are not left penniless after retiring from work.

Where does the wealth of a city like Adelaide come from? Many people work in huge factories building motorcars and other road vehicles. The two chief companies concerned are Chrysler's and General Motors-Holden. The vehicles built are sold not only in Adelaide itself but many are sent to the other large cities of Australia, although both Melbourne and Sydney have car factories also. As well as the automobile industry, Adelaide has factories making all sorts of electrical goods, like televisions and refrigerators, there are clothing and furniture workshops, printing and publishing houses, engineering works and a great many other businesses. At Port Adelaide also there are docks with warehouses, some of which are used for storing bales of wool and other products such as wheat which come from the farming country inland.

In earlier chapters cities which had serious problems of poverty were described. Adelaide has problems of a different kind.

Write some notes of your own describing the problems which may affect a prosperous city.

Compare Calcutta, Brasilia, and São Paulo (chapters 4 and 8). One of these is a planned city but already it has surprised its planners—the satellite towns have grown up unexpectedly. In the other cities unplanned growth has been too rapid, and the result has been poverty for many people, although there is also great wealth in these places. Can city planners, by careful thought, prevent such problems arising in future? Can planners see far enough into the future to avoid making serious mistakes?

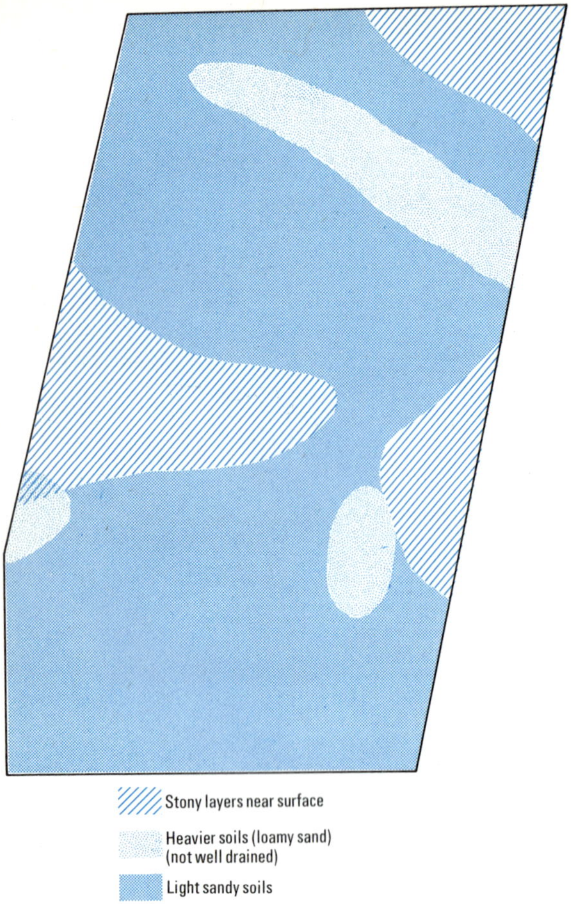

Fig. 84 Diagram showing soils on the Coats' farm

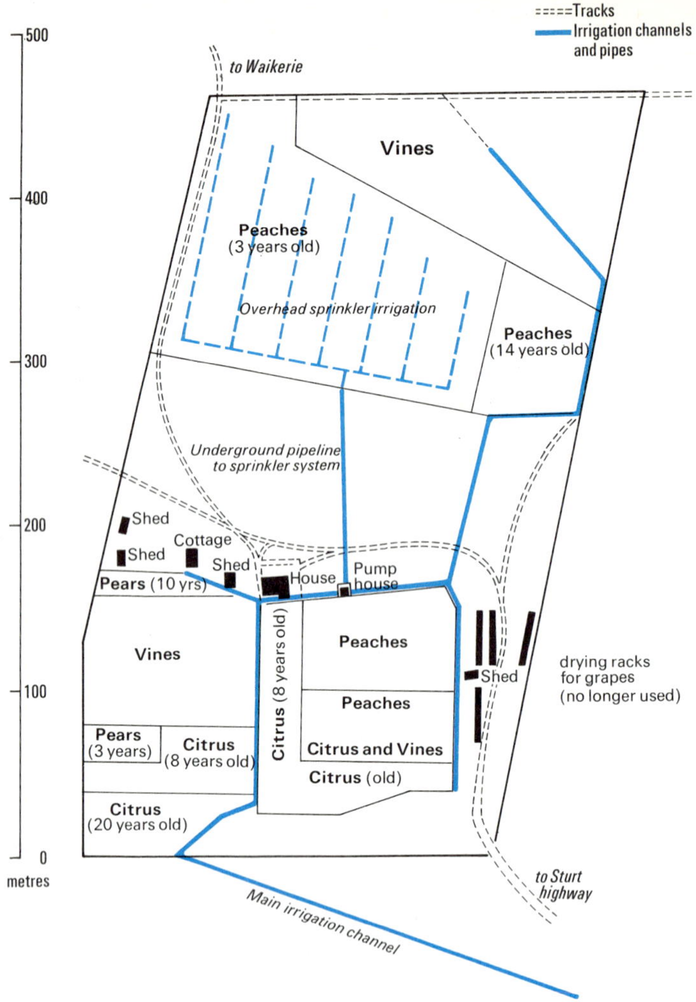

Fig. 85 Plan of a Waikerie fruit farm

10 Fruit Growers in South Australia

Photo. 106 Waikerie town from the air. The Coats' farm is visible on the left. Notice the great difference between land on the near side of the river, and that on the other side, which is not irrigated.

Fig. 85 is a plan of a fruit farm belonging to the Coats family in the Waikerie district of South Australia. See map on p. 121.

The average rainfall per annum of Waikerie is about 250 mm. The temperatures in summer frequently exceed 40°C. This is far too dry and hot for most crops; maps of climate show Waikerie as being a semi-desert region. Waikerie is far from being a desert. It is the centre of a prosperous fruit growing area. The farm plan and the chart (Figs. 85 and 87) show what fruits are grown. Notice on the chart that for each crop the monthly water need is given—peaches in January, for example, need the equivalent of 222 mm of rain. (This is the amount that would cover the land 222 mm deep if none of the water soaked away or dried up.) In January, Waikerie farms usually receive only about 13 mm of rain—this is the hottest season of the year (southern hemisphere), so that most of the rain water evaporates.

Study the chart carefully. Is there any month in the year when the average rainfall is enough to supply the fruit growers' needs?

The town of Waikerie, like many others in Australia, depends entirely on water taken from the River Murray.

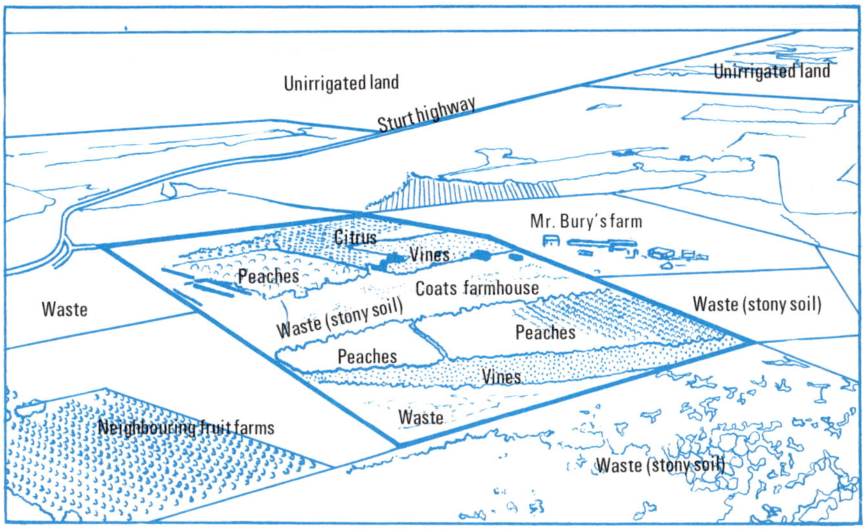

Fig. 86 A sketch of the Coats' farm made from an aerial photograph, with explanation.

	Jan	Feb	Mar	Apr	May	June	July	Aug	Sept	Oct	Nov	Dec	Annual total
Peaches	harvest spray	harvest	harvest		pruning	pruning	pruning	pruning weeding	pruning	thinning spray	thinning spray		
water need	222 mm	222 mm	44 mm	44 mm			44 mm	44 mm	44 mm	57 mm	178 mm	222 mm	1121 mm
Apricot	harvest				spray	pruning	pruning spray	pruning weeding		spray		harvest	
water need	165 mm	165 mm	44 mm	44 mm			57 mm	83 mm	165 mm	222 mm	222 mm	89 mm	1256 mm
Citrus (oranges, lemons, grapefruit)		spray			harvest (oranges) fertilizer	harvest (oranges)	harvest (oranges) fertilizer	harvest (grape-fruit, lemons, oranges)	harvest (oranges) fertilizer spray	harvest (oranges)		fertilizer spray	
water need	114 mm	114 mm	57 mm	44 mm	44 mm	19 mm	44 mm	19 mm	19 mm	44 mm	114mm	114mm	632mm
Vines (grapes)	spray		harvest				pruning	fertilizer pruning weeding	spray		spray	spray	
water need	203 mm	165 mm	38 mm	70 mm	51 mm			44 mm	44 mm	51 mm	146 mm	203 mm	1015 mm
Average rainfall	13 mm	23 mm	13 mm	14 mm	22 mm	29 mm	19 mm	27 mm	26 mm	24 mm	17 mm	21 mm	248 mm

Fig. 87 Chart showing average rainfall and the water need of the fruit

Irrigation

The map (Fig. 88) shows how the Murray, with its great tributary the Darling, rises in the mountains of the Great Dividing Range close to the eastern coasts of Australia, and flows generally westwards to the sea about 100 kilometres south-east of Adelaide. At Waikerie there is a large pumphouse by the river which raises the water 39 metres to fill the main irrigation channels, forcing it through large pipelines, some of which run underground through the built-up area of the town; others are on the surface.

Use the map (Fig. 89) to trace the route taken by water going to the Coats' farm. The farm plan and photographs show how the water is used on the land. A system of open, concrete-lined channels with small sluice gates carries the water to each part of the farm, and a large area is served by an overhead sprinkler system. Two methods of irrigation are used in Waikerie. The open furrow method is cheap but involves much hard work by the farmer. From the sluices

Photo. 107 The pumping station and ferry at Waikerie. Notice the pipes leading from the river to the pumps.

Fig. 88 Irrigation areas of south-east Australia

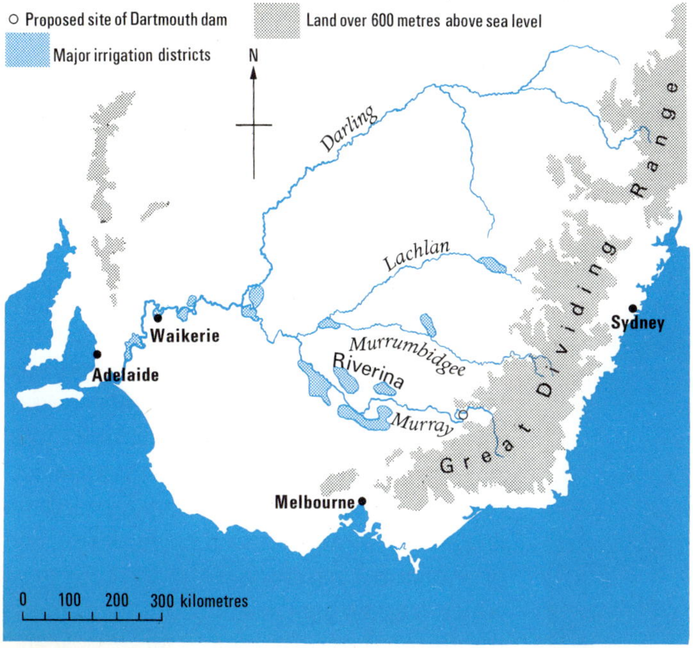

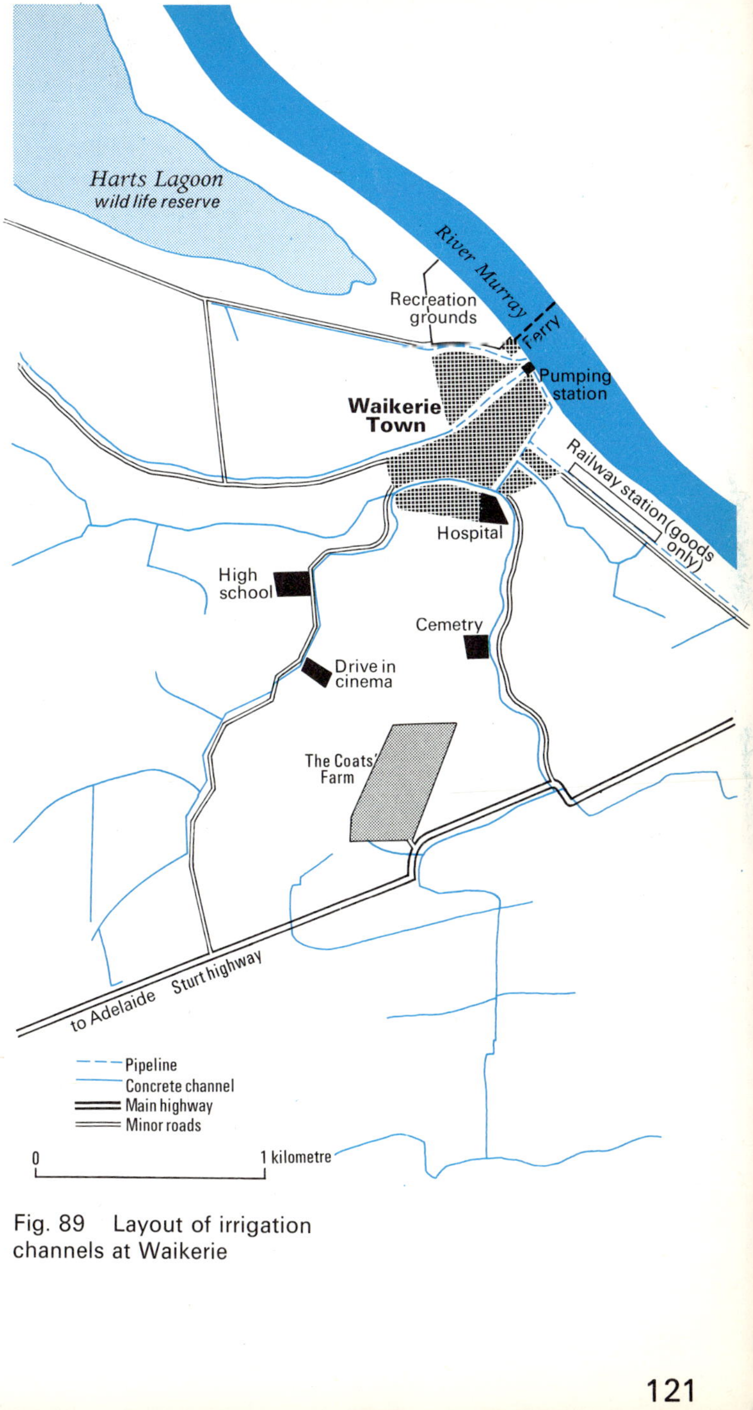

Fig. 89 Layout of irrigation channels at Waikerie

Photo. 108 One of the main irrigation channels in Waikerie. A typical sluice gate leading to a peach orchard is shown in the foreground. To open the gate the farmer raises the steel plate which can be seen above the sluice.

Photo. 109 Furrow irrigation of vines

in the open channels he must dig a whole series of shallow trenches to take the water along the rows of trees or vines. He must plan his farm carefully so that water can flow downwards in these channels to reach every tree. When his turn for water comes, he must be on the spot to open the sluices and he must keep the earth furrows open. He or his men must arrange for each part of the land to get the right quantity of water.

Each farmer is allowed a fair share of the water pumped from the river, and each has to pay for the water taken. Sometimes the water reaches the farm at night, and whatever the time the farmer must be ready for it. The flow may continue for twelve or more hours, after which the sluices must be closed so that water in the main channel can flow to the next property. A disadvantage of the open furrow system is that a great deal of the water is wasted. Much of it evaporates from the furrows, and more tends to soak away into the soil away from the tree roots.

The overhead sprinkler system costs much more to install. On many farms there is a small pumphouse. The underground pipe system carries the water to the sprays, which may be seen in many of the orchards standing three or four metres above

Photo. 110 Picking peaches on the Coats' farm. Some sorting of poor fruit is done at this stage.

Photo. 111 Sorting peaches in the orchard. Poor fruit is dumped on the ground; the sound peaches are put into large wooden bins for carting away to the cannery.

ground. When the sprinklers are turned on the orchard is covered by an even fall of water and all the farmer needs to do is to turn the motor on and off at the appropriate time.

The chart (Fig. 87) shows the work of the Waikerie farms from month to month. From this chart, can you say which month of the year is the holiday period? Even during this time, notice that some irrigation must still be done. Remembering that in the southern hemisphere the seasons are different from those in Europe, which fruits are picked in summer and which in winter?

Picking peaches

During the fruit picking period Mr. Coats employs sometimes as many as twenty men to help with the harvest. The men are paid for each bin of fruit filled. The bins for peaches are large wooden boxes about one metre deep and 1·5 metres long by 1·2 metres wide, and each picker fills one bin at a time, chalking his name on the side. He is not allowed to handle the fruit roughly, since this causes bruising; he must take care when picking not to take unripe fruit or fruit which has been damaged by insects or other pests.

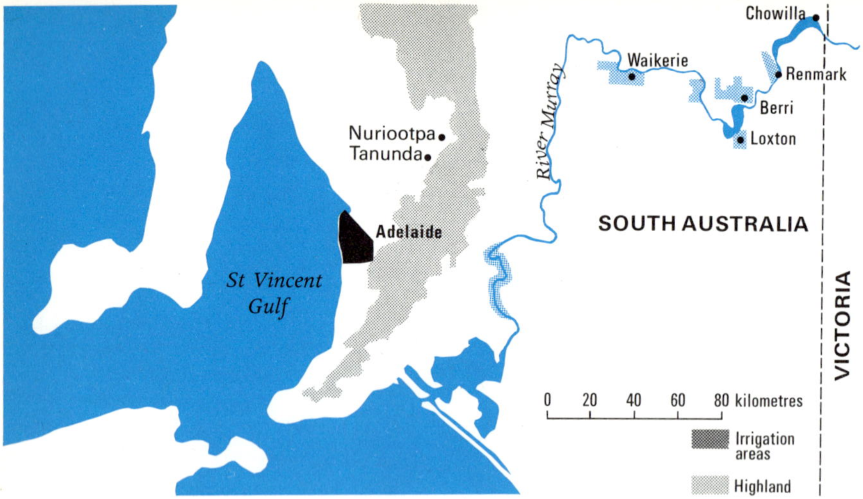

Fig. 90 Map showing the position of Waikerie and Adelaide

Most of the peaches from Waikerie go for canning, and the cannery which is in the town of Berri (see Fig. 90) will not accept peaches below a certain size; usually 6 centimetres in diameter. The pickers throw down to the ground any fruit which is smaller than this. After filling their picking bags they descend the ladder and tip the fruit onto a metal tray attached to the side of the bin, and sort it out again, throwing out still more poor fruit. They have a small piece of wood or heavy fibreboard with a hole in it—fruit which will pass easily through the hole is thrown away. Usually the pickers can judge the fruit without using this gauge.

Work begins very early in the morning soon after dawn, but the ripeness of the fruit is judged by its colour and the pickers have to wait for the light to be strong enough to distinguish green fruit from the yellow or orange of a ripe peach. As the day goes on the heat increases and usually they stop work early in the afternoon; by then experienced ones will have filled three bins each.

Pests

Sometimes the picking is more difficult, if the trees have been affected by a pest for example, the amount of damaged fruit may be much more than usual. In 1968 and 1969, the whole of the Waikerie area was plagued by millions of tiny black flies, known as Rutherglen flies, which attacked both the peach and the apricot crop. Wherever these flies settled on the fruit they left small punctures in the skin and on cutting the peaches or apricots for canning many small brown marks were found. Some farmers lost more than half their usual crop in that season. Fortunately most pests can be controlled by spraying the trees with insecticides and other substances. The spraying equipment is usually towed around the orchards by tractors; the men operating it have to wear protective clothing since some of the pesticides are very dangerous.

Many different sprays are used, each one is intended to give protection against some particular pests or disease in the trees, but sometimes, as with the Rutherglen fly, the farmers are taken by surprise. Occasionally,

Photo. 112 Rex Coats inspecting his orange trees. This land was sprayed two months ago to kill the weeds. The weeds are dead, but now the chemical weedkiller has reached the tree roots. The weed killer in this orchard was evidently mixed too strong, and the leaves on the trees are turning slightly yellow. Rex fears that next year's crop will suffer.

some of the farmers employ an aerial crop sprayer.

Fertilizing

Apart from spraying against disease, the farmers must fertilize their land properly. Fertilizers are usually spread mechanically —a tractor tows the spreading machine along between the rows of trees or vines, scattering the powdered material on the ground. The irrigation water later washes it down into the soil.

Weeding

If weeds are allowed to grow unchecked they draw much of the nourishment from the soil, and the fertilizers are wasted. The usual method of weeding is to cultivate the soil regularly, using a disc harrow or other machine, but in recent years some farmers have been spraying their land with weed killing substances, which is cheaper than cultivation.

Pruning

Pruning and thinning fruit on the trees is a lengthy task which can only be done by hand, by experienced men. Every tree or vine is worked over carefully; the branches are trimmed to encourage the best growth and to cut out old wood or diseased limbs. The farmers has to balance quantity of fruit against quality. A tree that is allowed to grow too many peaches will produce a large weight of crop but far too many of the peaches will be small and below standard.

Oranges

Picking the oranges is fairly similar to the peach picking, though of course at a cooler time of year. Citrus trees need little pruning once they are growing properly.

Photo. 113 Mr. Elliot, another Waikerie farmer, still dries some of his grapes. He and Mr. Coats are shown here inspecting the raisins after two weeks' drying on the racks.

Photo. 114 Rex Coats inspects his vine crop. These sultanas are about two weeks away from harvest. They will be sold to a winery.

Vines

The vines produce their grapes in large bunches, which are cut off by the pickers with secateurs and put into tins. Many farms in the Waikerie area have large grape-drying racks. These are wooden or steel framed structures with roofs of corrugated iron and layers of chicken wire on which the grapes can be spread (Photo 113). After two days on the racks the grapes are sprayed with a chemical that speeds up the drying and then allowed to dry for several weeks to produce the familiar small dark brown blueish raisins, currants or sultanas. However, in Waikerie, at the present time most of these racks are unused since the grapes are sold after picking to be made into wine. There is a distillery and winery in Waikerie, but most of the crop goes in large lorries to Nuriootpa or Tanunda and other towns in the same area, where there are many large and famous wine making companies (Fig. 90).

Planning

Fruit trees are unlike other farm crops because they do not have to be re-sown or planted every year. Instead the farmer must plan many years ahead.

Photo. 115 Pears drying in the sun on a farm neighbouring the Coats property. Mr. Bury, the owner, dries most of his fruit and has spent a great deal of money on the special equipment needed. His house, seen in the background, is a typical South Australian farm house, with wide, shady verandahs, rainwater tank and pleasant garden.

The larger trees are much more complicated. Often a tree is produced by grafting. The root of one variety of orange, for example, is grafted to the stem of another, and the farmer has to judge which type of root stock he should plant. Different root stocks require different types of soil, and Fig. 84 on page 118 shows that, on the Coats' farm, there are three main types of soil. The parts of the farm where layers of limestone lie within a few centimetres of the surface are not suitable for any crop and these have been left unplanted.

Vines can grow quite well on fairly stony soils and the farm plan shows that the vines are fairly close to the stony areas although the surface soil is sandy. The sheet stone of the waste area continues under the vineyards about a metre down. Peaches require a good soil free of lime, and deep enough for the tree roots to go well down. The citrus trees can grow well on most soils providing their roots are not too damp, so they must be planted on well-drained soils. Compare the soil map of the farm with the layout of the different crops and notice how the trees are arranged, to take advantage of the best land. Every farmer in Waikerie has similar problems.

Waikerie

Waikerie town is quite small with about 3000 people and depends almost entirely on the fruit-growing industry. In the town there are all the shops and other services needed by the farmers and farm workers. There are several schools and a kindergarten, a hospital, churches, garages, and a large fruit-packing shed which provides work for many of the local girls, as well as some who come to the district from other parts of Australia. The railway that enters the town from the south carries only goods, and during the summer most of the trains carry wheat away from the town. Beyond the irrigated region there are many very large wheat farms. The wheat farmers bring their crop in lorries to Waikerie where the grain is stored in two tall, concrete silos, to be loaded onto the train for carriage to Port Adelaide. However, Waikerie is only one of a great many collecting points for the wheat. The town stands close to the Sturt Highway, which provides a route for the peach and apricot crop to go to Berri for canning and for the grapes to go to the distilleries in the other direction.

Photo. 116 The Waikerie 'drive in' cinema. Note the pedestals and the large screen. (A typical, tall television aerial is visible in the background.) The existence of a 'drive in' cinema indicates quite a lot of things about the climate of the district.

Photo. 117 The River Murray at Waikerie. Notice the 30 metre limestone cliff. Water for irrigation has to be raised to this height. The land on the left of this picture is not suitable for farming. The soil is salty and liable to flooding.

Recreation

Three kilometres east of the town, on a flat but very stony area which cannot be used for fruit, there is a small aerodrome. Light aeroplanes sometimes call here for fuel, and two small air charter crop spraying and pilot training companies operate. However, the main use of the airfield is as a base for a large gliding club.

The Murray river provides other sport in the district. Many of the young men go water-skiing, boating, and fishing, and some of the riverside lagoons provide duck shooting, though Harts Lagoon, nearest to the town, is a sanctuary for the black swans and other large birds like pelicans and ibis which are common along the Murray. In the wild country north of the river parties sometimes go hunting. The town itself has many different kinds of clubs and societies, and there is a 'drive in' cinema. At the 'drive in' motorists arrive in their cars and drive up to a parking place where a small loudspeaker attached to a pedestal can be hooked onto a side window of the car. The screen is viewed through the windscreen.

Use the chart and the other information given in this chapter to make a list of the different jobs which are open to people in Waikerie. Don't overlook 'service' industries like transport, shopkeepers, etc.

Further up the Murray, and in Victoria and New South Wales, there are other, larger towns and irrigation districts which are very similar to Waikerie, although often different crops are grown. Fruit and other produce from these riverside towns is sold to the large cities, Sydney, Melbourne, and Adelaide itself, and much is also exported to Japan and England.

Floods

Trouble can come in two ways. In the winter of 1956 the Murray received far more than its usual quantity of water from the heavy rainfall and snow melt in the mountains, and its large tributary, the Darling, also at this time was at its peak flow. Great floods followed all the way down the Murray and many of the lower-lying irrigated lands were covered several metres deep in flowing water. Whole orchards were destroyed and many houses were swept away. At Waikerie the pump-house itself was flooded and many of the farms below the cliffs were destroyed.

Some of the farmers near Harts Lagoon saved themselves by working together, day and night, to build a long earthen embankment on the south side of the lagoon. After toiling all day as the water rose, they managed to keep a few centimetres ahead of the river by nightfall. The next morning the water would be lapping the top of their dam, and another full day's work with tractors, bulldozers, and anything that could be pressed into service, enabled them to gain another few centimetres. This desperate struggle continued for nearly a month before the river gradually began to fall again.

Irrigating high land

In spite of such efforts, many farmers in the Waikerie area lost almost everything they had, and after the flood found their land completely ruined. To assist them to recover, a new area of land to the west of the town was developed for irrigation. The chief difficulty with this new project was that the land was much higher above the river than the rest, and although this meant it would be well clear of any future floods, it also meant that a completely new pumping station would be needed, and the water would have to be raised over 60 metres. The cost of water to the farmers would be more than usual, and it was not sure that, with these extra costs, they would be able to make a living. The new pumping station was built at Ramco (Fig. 91) and the Golden Heights irrigation area was laid out, and the land offered for sale to Waikerie farmers. The scheme proved to be very successful, for the area was one of good, deep, and fertile soils so the extra cost of the water was balanced by better crops. Since 1960 further very large extensions to the irrigated area have taken place—in 1961 Sunlands South, a year later Sunland North, and in 1965 Ramco Heights.

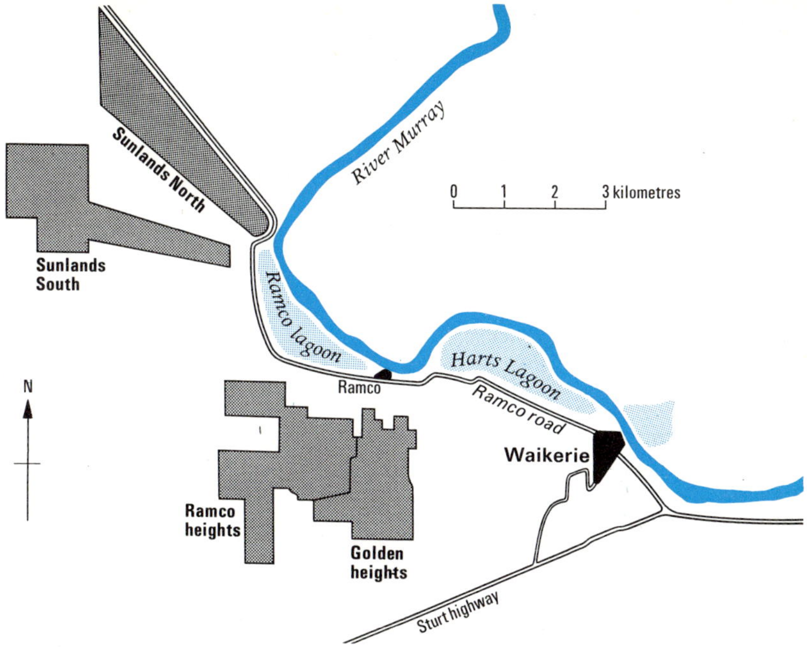

Fig. 91 Newly irrigated areas around Waikerie

All these new developments followed a great flood when there was suddenly far too much water in the river. But sometimes exactly the opposite can occur. In a drought year, the Murray dwindles in size and the irrigation schemes run into serious trouble if there is not enough water. An orange tree takes 8 years to grow to full size. If an orchard is killed through lack of water in one year, the farmer gets no crop from this land for several more years afterwards. So far no such severe drought has struck Waikerie, though in some years recently after long dry spells the farmers have found their trees damaged because the river water becomes too salty. Waikerie is one of the last areas to receive the water. The larger irrigation schemes farther up the river, in a dry year, could use all the water, leaving those downstream without. Fortunately there are agreements between the governments of South Australia and the other river states (New South Wales and Victoria) to ensure fair sharing. But the possibility of disastrous drought is still present. To prevent this, the best method would be to build one or more new dams on the river, to store water in the wet years for use in dry periods. Work on a new dam to be built at Chowilla, close to the borders of South Australia and Victoria, had actually begun when it was decided instead to site the new dam in the mountains at Dartmouth on the river Mitta Mitta, a tributary of the Murray. Water from this new reservoir, when completed, will be released to serve all the irrigated areas of the Murray as required. In this way it is hoped that the drought problem will be overcome for many years ahead. Until the new dam is built, further development of the irrigated lands at Waikerie is unlikely.

For discussion

On the whole would you describe Waikerie as a wealthy or poor town? Do you suppose anyone in this area is ever actually short of food?

Is Waikerie a commercial or subsistence farming town?

The population of Waikerie is increasing. Can you think of any reason why too rapid a growth might lead to poverty?

Poverty in Australia

Photo. 118 The township of Oodnadatta seen from the railway water tower

The small town of Oodnadatta is 1100 km. north-east of Adelaide in South Australia. It is in a desert region. There is a railway station, a small hospital, a police station, a couple of shops and a school. The airfield outside the town is used as a base for the famous flying doctor service. The map (Fig. 92) shows the layout of the town and marks the position of the water tower from which Photo. 118 was taken. The photographer had to climb the tower to get this picture since there is no high ground anywhere nearby. The tower belongs to the railway company and was used in the days of steam trains to supply the locomotives. The water comes from a deep bore hole to the reservoir near the town and then it is taken by pipeline to the tower. Unfortunately this water is not fit to drink since it is salty.

For drinking water the people of the town collect rain from their house roofs. Although rain falls rarely there is usually enough to keep going.

Most of the town's people have good houses to live in. They may be hospital workers or railway employees. There is not much entertainment in the town itself, but it is fairly easy to fly to Alice Springs.

Fig. 92 Oodnadatta township

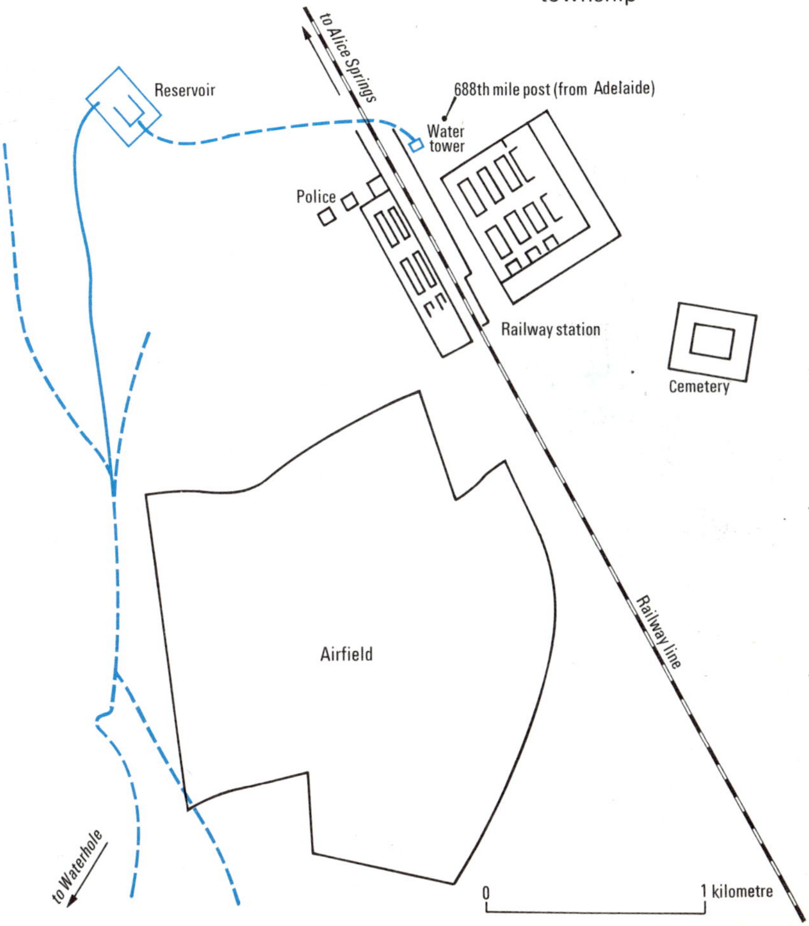

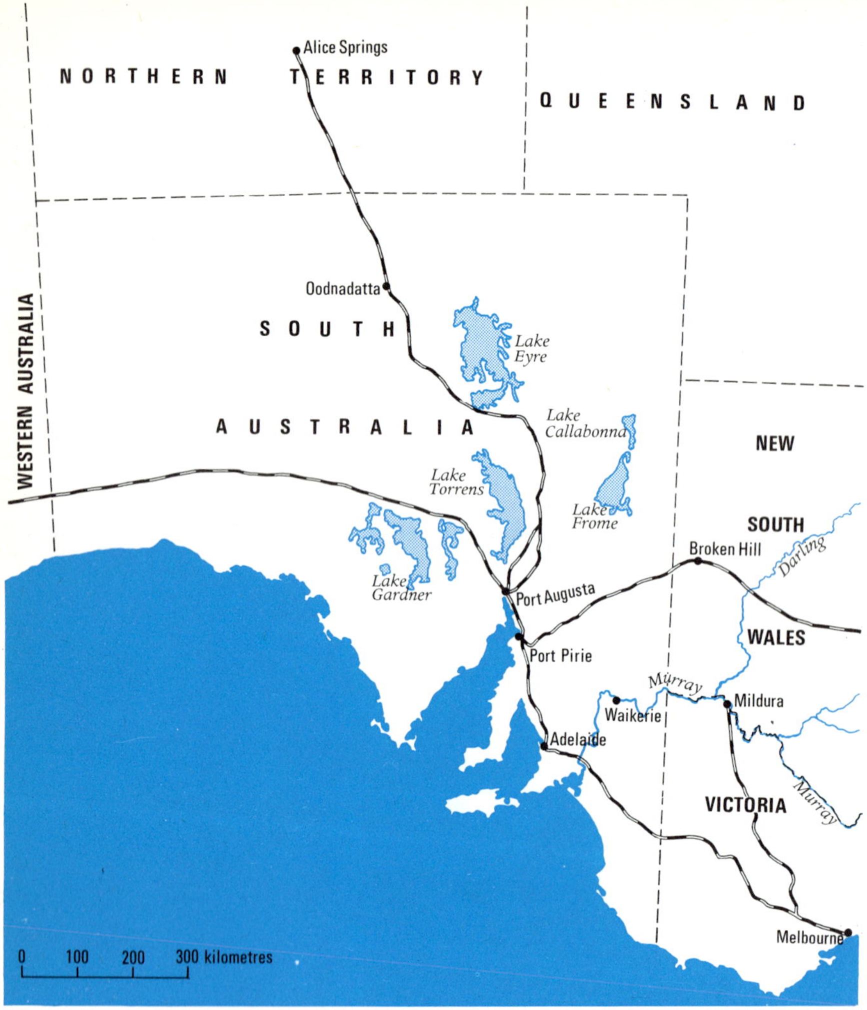

Fig. 93 The position of Oodnadatta in South Australia

Photo. 119, however, shows that some people at Oodnadatta do not live in houses at all. Just outside the town there are several reserves for the Aboriginals, the people who lived in Australia for thousands of years before the white man discovered the continent. They were stone-age people, hunting for food with weapons such as spears, throwing sticks and boomerangs. Agriculture was unknown to them. They wandered from place to place within their tribal lands. They had, and still do have, their own languages, customs and religious beliefs. In many places there are brilliant and beautiful cave paintings done by Aboriginal artists; they also produce sculpture and music of kinds unknown anywhere else in the world, with dances and secret ceremonies which are rarely shown to strangers. Life was always desperately hard, but it was simple.

The arrival of the European settlers with their machinery and new ideas upset this ancient way of life for most of the tribes. To begin with they were often treated very cruelly by the newcomers. Nowadays the government tries to understand them better and encourages the Aboriginals to fit into the life of the white man. Many Aboriginals work as stockmen on big cattle and sheep stations. In Adelaide some work for regular wages in factories. However, many Aboriginals do not want to adopt the ways of white men. They try to keep their old customs and skills and often distrust or misunderstand even the people who try to help them. Yet of course they are affected by civilisation. Such things as corrugated iron, oil drums, cardboard boxes, car tyres,

Photo. 119 A humpy with many factory-made articles lying about—a baby's cot, an old bedstead, oil drums, food cans, utensils and boxes. None of these were part of the old Aboriginal way of life.

Photo. 120 Humpies shaded by small trees close to Oodnadatta

Photo. 121 An Aboriginal workman wearing modern clothing, chipping stones to make a sharp tool

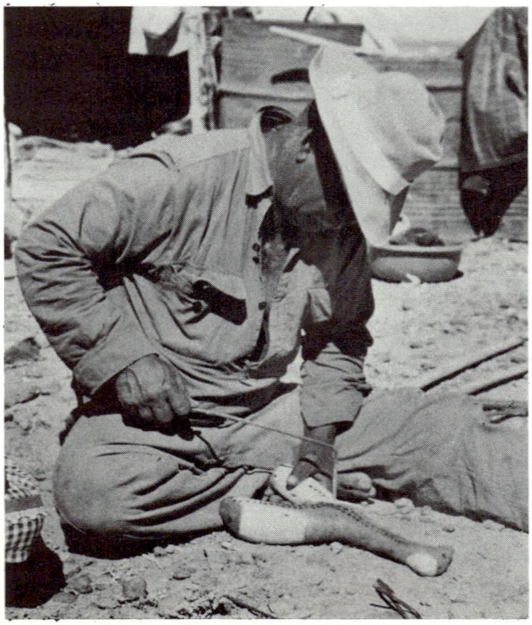

Photo. 122 Carving a wooden Emu for sale to tourists. The style of carving is very ancient, but the metal tool is modern.

etc., are used at Oodnadatta in all kinds of ways alongside ancient customs which were developed in another age. Carvings and sculptures which used to have great importance in religion are now often made and sold to tourists for cash: the Aboriginal who is still able to chip a stone to create a sharp cutting tool is likely to use a factory-made metal knife for his normal work, and he will buy, if he can afford it, clothing and tinned food from a shop instead of going without, or hunting. His children will attend school and learn to read and write, he will probably be able to drive a car and if he is sick he will receive help from a doctor. The Aboriginal stands between two ways of life—his old one has been destroyed, but, in many cases, he has not yet fully understood the new way.

Compare the Aboriginal 'humpies' shown in this section with the poor housing of Calcutta and the shanty towns of Brasilia or São Paulo. Discuss with your class and teacher the ways in which the Aboriginals' old way of life has been changed. Would it be fair to say they were 'poor' before the white man came to Australia? Are they 'poorer' now than before?

Postscript

The example areas described in this book show that wealth and poverty are to be found, often side by side, in many areas of the southern continents and India. In rural areas there are great contrasts between subsistence farming and commercial farming. The subsistence farmer depends on his crops for food; if the crops fail by reason of climate or because of bad farming methods, he and his family go hungry. But commercial farmers must be able to send their produce away by road, rail or sea to be sold for cash. If there is no means of transporting the crop, or if no one wants to buy it, they, too, can face poverty. And again, crop failure can lead to disaster.

Every large city mentioned in the book is growing rapidly. The main reason in every case is the immigration of people from country areas, although there is usually some 'natural increase' also. In Singapore and Adelaide, although not everyone is rich, there are few bad slums, and on the whole building has kept pace with growth. But in Bombay, Calcutta, and other Indian cities, many thousands of people have not even a roof to sleep under, and in São Paulo, the richest city in Brazil, there are slums, and building of flats, roads, drains, etc., is lagging behind constantly as more people pour in. People come to live in a city because there they hope to find work.

Making plans for many years ahead, as in the case of Brasilia, is one possible way of ensuring that new cities will grow without slums arising—but planners sometimes make mistakes. No-one is really able to look far enough ahead to be sure of avoiding difficulties in later years. Even when the plan is good, people do not always want to do as the planners require; at Brasilia new towns have appeared which were never intended.

Not only in the southern continents, but everywhere in the world similar problems arise. Sometimes the reasons are obvious when farmers suffer crop failure or cities experience unexpectedly rapid growth. At other times the explanations for poverty are much more difficult to discover. There may be combinations of several factors, natural and social, which react on one another. The solution is rarely easy in such cases.

In your further studies and reading about other parts of the world, keep in mind the things you have learned about wealth and poverty, and try to work out how improvements can be made.

Index

Aboriginals, 132–4
Carving, 132–4
Cave paintings, 132
Humpies, 133
Accra, 22–3
Adelaide, 107–17
African climatic zones, 13
Agra, 49
Ahmedabad, 51
Ako sombo, 26
Allahabad, 49
Aluminium industry, 24–5
Amanat River, 60
Aminbhavi village, 74–5
Ashanti, 20
Banana growing, 39
Bangalore, 51
Berri, 124
Bihar, 56–71
Bombay, 51
Brahman caste, 72–3
Brasilia, 96–103
Building materials, 80
Bustees, 52
Calcutta, 41–5
Redevelopment, 52–3
Canberra plan, 104
Caste system, 72–3
Chandigarh, 53
Chile, 86–91
Chinese in Singapore, 82
Chowilla dam project, 130
Citrus growing, 125
Cocoa, 28–9, 89
Collective farms, 89
Cuncumen district, 86–7
Darling River, 120
Dartmouth Dam project, 130
Delhi, 51
Detroit, 107
Diseases in Nangodi, 15
Drought
Bihar, 67–8
Murray irrigation areas, 130
Dry season in Nangodi, 12
Electronic industry, Ghana, 26
Expressways, 115
Factories, 71, 117
Farmer training schools, 90–1
Fertilizers, 125
Fishing industry, Ghana, 26
Floods
Australia, 128–9
Bihar, 65–6
Forest
Bihar, 59–60
Ghana, 19
Freeways, 114
Fruit growing, 119–21
Fundos in Chile, 88
Gandak River, 64–5
Ganges River, 50–1
Ghana, 8–29
Gold mining, 20
Migration, 27
Rainfall, 19
River transport, 19
Traffic flow, 22
Golden Heights irrigation area, 129
Ground nuts, 11
Guinea Fowl, 11
Haciendas in S America, 88–9
Hinduism, 72–3
Houses
Adelaide, 116
Chile, 86
India, 72–5
Nangodi, 16–17
Singapore, 76–85
Housing statistics, 46
Hunger, 10
Hyderabad, 51
Hydro-electric power, 25
India, 56–75
Industrialization, 70–1
Iron and steel industry, 70–1
Migration, 49
Rainfall, 60–1
Slums, 44–9
Street dwellers, 44
Insecticide, 35
Irrigation, 119–20
Islamabad plan, 105
Jamshedphur, 53–4, 70–1
Kampong House, 80
Kanpur, 46–8
Kenya, 30–9
Kericho, Kenya, 37
Kikuyu, Kenya, 38
Kosi River, 64–5
Kshatriyas caste, 72
Kumasi, 20
Levees, 64–5
Light, William, 107–8
Lucknow, 49
Madras, 51
Masai, 35
Millet, 11
Minais Gerais, 99
Mombasa, 30
Monsoon, 41, 60–2
Monsoon lands of Asia, 66
Motorways, 114
Murray River, 107, 120–9
Nairobi, 30–1
Nangodi, 8–17
Rainfall, 12–13
Red Volta River, 14
Weight tables, 9–10
New Delhi, 105
Oodnadatta, 131–4
Oranges, 125
Owner cultivators, 88–9
Oxford, 107
Patna, 58
Peaches, 123
Pests of fruit trees, 124
Pig farming, 84
Planning
Adelaide, 106–18
Brasilia, 98–9
Calcutta, 52
Plans of cities, 104–5
Population
Adelaide, 112
Bihar, 56, 58
Kanpur, 47
Nangodi, 14
Singapore, 82–4
Port Adelaide, 117
Pruning, 125
Pyrethrum, 28
Railways
Ghana, 20
Kenya, 30
Ramco irrigation area, 129
Re-settlement, Volta scheme, 25–7
Rice growing, 62–3
Rio de Janeiro, 98
River control, 70
Roads, 18–19, 112
Sahara desert, 12–13
Santiago, 92–3
São Paulo, 92–7
Savanna, 14, 19
Sekondi, 20–3
Singapore, 76–85
Winds, 79
Temperatures, 77–80
Sisal, 39
Soil erosion, 91
Subsistence economy, 64
Sudras caste, 72
Sunlands irrigation area, 129
Surf boats, 23–4
Takoradi, 23
Tanks, water storage, 60
Tarkwa, 20
Tea growing, 36–7
Tema, 23–4
Timber industry (Ghana), 20
Untouchables caste, 72–3
Uttar Pradesh, 49–51
Vaisyas caste, 72
Varanasi, 49
Villages, India, 56–65, 72–5
Vines, 126
Volta River scheme, 24–6
Waikerie, 118–29
Wattle bark, 33
Wells in Bihar, 68
Wine industry, 126
Winnowing grain, 11, 62